Popular
Italian
Cookery

Popular Italian Cookery

by Marion Howells

Octopus Books

Photographs on pages 2, 71, 98, 114, 119 by courtesy of Syndication International.

Photographs on pages 26, 35, 42, 47, 50, 54, 55, 58, 70, 75, 90, 91, 95, 99, 106, 118, 123 by courtesy of Paf International.

Frontispiece: Chicken breasts in sauce. Soup pastas. Risotto. Lasagne. Tagliatelli.

First published 1972 by
Octopus Books Limited
59 Grosvenor Street, London W1

ISBN 7064 0067 4

© 1972 Octopus Books Limited

Produced by Mandarin Publishers

Printed in Hong Kong

Contents

Weights and measures   6

Introduction.   7

Antipasti and Salads   13

Soups   31

Vegetables   40

Pasta, Pizza and Rice.   60

Sauces.   81

Fish   86

Meat and Poultry.   96

Desserts 112

Index. 127

Weights and Measures

All measurements in this book are based on Imperial weights and measures, with American equivalents given in parenthesis.

Measurements in *weight* in the Imperial and American system are the same.
Measurements in *volume* are different, and the following table shows the equivalents:

Spoon measurements

Imperial	U.S.
1 teaspoon (5ml.)	$1\frac{1}{4}$ teaspoons
1 tablespoon (20ml.)	$1\frac{1}{4}$ tablespoons (abbrev: T)

Level spoon measurements are used in all the recipes.

Liquid measurements

1 Imperial pint	20 fluid ounces
1 American pint	16 fluid ounces
1 American cup.	8 fluid ounces

Introduction

Italy

Does that name conjure up for you memories of Lasagne, Osso Buco, Saltimbocco, Ravioli, Veal Escalopes Milanese, Frito Misto or Zabaglione, to say nothing of delicious cheese and wines.

The characteristics of Italian cookery are simplicity, the high quality of the ingredients and the freshness of the flavour, together with the delightful colour of so many regional dishes. The bright red of dishes with tomato sauce, the pinkish fish soups, colourful pizzas, the green lasagne – all are a delight to the eye.

One of the great joys of eating in Italy is the abundance of fresh fruit and vegetables. Italian housewives shop daily as a rule and make the best possible use of fresh local produce. With one or two exceptions, vegetables are not served as an accompaniment to meat dishes, but treated as a separate course – generally as an hors d'oeuvre or antipasti – and what a wealth of vegetables there are from which to choose.

Young broad beans are often eaten raw as a first course, as are red and green peppers, artichokes, aubergines and courgettes (zucchini). French beans, spinach, broccoli, fennel and mushrooms are often dressed with olive oil and lemon juice and served as a salad.

Each region has its own specialities and this is sometimes confusing as they all have their own names for dishes which are common to all parts of the country.

Tomatoes, which feature in so many Italian dishes, are grown in most regions. They are large, sweet and rich in flavour. Unless a recipe calls for fresh tomatoes, it is often better to use the canned peeled Italian ones, especially in making sauces, soups, and stews.

Concentrated tomato paste or purée features quite often in Italian dishes and this can be bought quite easily in tubes.

Pine nuts are used in a number of meat and game dishes. They come from the Stone Pine, are creamy in colour and have a slightly oily flavour. They are also used in biscuits, like macaroons, and are very good if salted and served with cocktails. There is no real substitute for pine nuts, but they can often be bought in shops which specialize in vegetarian or health foods and, of course, in Italian food stores.

Chestnuts are used in large quantities too – for soups, as a vegetable and also for rich luscious sweets, including marron glacé. In October there is a special chestnut festival in Senise in the south of Italy.

You may have noticed strings of dried mushrooms hanging up in Italian provision shops. The Italians often use these in soups, stews and sauces. They should be soaked for about fifteen minutes in warm water and added to the other ingredients for the last twenty minutes of the cooking. If over cooked, they tend to become flabby and lose their flavour.

The grey green foliage of the olive trees is an essential feature of the Italian landscape, and olive oil is used a great deal in Italian cooking. People sometimes complain that Italian food is too 'oily', but when the best oil is properly used this is not justified, for the food is rich, fragrant and delicious.

Some of the Italian oil sold outside Italy is very much refined and does not have the full flavour of the best olive oil, but it is quite good for cooking. The famous oil from Lucca in Tuscany is generally available and it is well worth using this for salads.

Cheeses

If you have been to Italy and wandered round the market stalls and shops, you will no doubt have been surprised at the extensive range of cheeses of all shapes and sizes. With the exception of France, Italy has a greater variety than any other country. Relatively few are exported in any quantity, but in many of the Italian food shops and delicatessens you will find a very fair selection.

Cheese plays a large part in Italian cookery and you will find Parmesan, Ricotta and Mozzarella mentioned in many of the recipes in this book.

Parmesan
often referred to as grana on account of its coarse texture, is made from skimmed milk and should be at least two years old. Being hard it is very suitable for grating and is much used, in this form, for cooking, both for its flavour and because it never goes 'stringy' when cooked. It is more economical to buy it by the piece and grate it freshly yourself when the flavour is also better.

Mozzarella

is a soft cheese originally made from buffalo's milk, but, the buffalo being used less and less, the cheese is being replaced by Scamorza, made from cow's milk. It melts easily at a low temperature and so is very useful in cooking. If it is to be eaten raw, it must be absolutely fresh and almost dripping with its own buttermilk. If you are not able to obtain Mozzarella cheese, Bel Paese could be substituted.

Ricotta

is a soft, unsalted curd cheese made from ewe's milk. In southern Italy and in Rome particularly, it is eaten with sugar or salt and cinnamon, but it is also used extensively in cooking. It has a fresh, delicately pungent flavour and the consistency is rather similar to cottage cheese.

Bel Paese

is a soft mild cheese. It is generally used as a table cheese, and the name means 'beautiful country'.

Gorgonzola

is a creamy blue-veined cheese, found mostly around Lombardy. It ranks as one of the most famous cheeses of the world. White Gorgonzola, which is practically unknown outside Italy, has a slightly bitter flavour and is greatly appreciated by Italian cheese connoisseurs.

The following are a few of the cheeses which can be bought in Italian food shops and in some delicatessens and supermarkets:

Fontina

is a rich cow's milk cheese with a delicate nutty flavour. It has tiny holes and is similar to a creamy Gruyère. It melts easily and is used in Fonduta or Cheese Fondue, one of the most famous dishes of Piedmont.

Provolone

is a sweet cow's milk cheese, which comes in various shapes and sizes. It is eaten raw when fresh, but as it ripens, the flavour becomes sharper and it hardens and is then used for cooking.

Pecorino

which is a general term for hard sharp cheese, is made from ewe's milk. It is eaten raw when fresh and is cooked when it is more mature.

Pecorino Romano

comes in many different shapes and sizes and has a strong flavour.

Pecorino Sardo

has a very tough rind.

Caciocavallo

is similar to Provolone. It came originally from the southern provinces but is now also made in northern Italy. It is mild, has a spicy tang when young and is used mostly as a table cheese, although it hardens as it matures and can then be grated.

Stracchino

is made from cow's milk and comes from Lombardy. It has a distinctive pungent flavour and a soft, slightly glutinous texture. Eat this while it is fresh, with a glass of red Chianti.

Herbs and Spices

The Italian housewife makes good use of herbs, but treats them with discretion.

Bay leaves

dried or fresh, are used for flavouring risotto and in casseroles of meat and fish.

Basil

has a spicy, aromatic scent and grows in profusion in southern Italy. It is used in tomato dishes and in soups, salads and sauces and no 'Pesto', (see page 85) can be made without it. Dried basil can sometimes be used as a substitute for the fresh herb but, unfortunately, not for making Pesto.

Borage

is not always easy to obtain. The flavour combines well with cucumber and in some parts of Italy it is used as a flavouring in salads and in a filling for ravioli.

Fennel

has an aniseed flavour and is the herb for fish and fish sauces.

Florence Fennel

is grown extensively in Italy and is eaten raw, thinly sliced and marinated in olive oil and lemon juice.

Garlic

contrary to common belief, is used with restraint in the best type of Italian cookery, although in and around Naples its use in flavouring soups and some spaghetti dishes may be a little more lavish.

Marjoram and Wild Oregano

are, with Basil, probably the most popular herbs in Italy. They are used for flavouring soups, fish, pasta, pizzas and stews.

Mint

is not used extensively in Italy. A fragrant wild mint which grows around Rome is used to flavour soups, salads and fish.

Parsley

Italian parsley has a strong flavour and the leaf is flat, thin and only slightly curly. It is used lavishly in soups, salads and stuffings for meat and various forms of ravioli.

Rosemary
has a strong, almost gingery flavour and is used with lamb and sucking pig.

Sage
is not used a great deal except in some veal dishes and always in the famous Saltimbocca, where a leaf of sage is tucked between the veal and ham (see page 100).

Saffron
is made from the dried stigmas of a certain type of crocus. It is very expensive to buy, even in Italy, but this is not surprising, as it elleged that 70,000 stigmas are required to make 1 lb. of saffron and there are only three stigmas on each flower. However, a little goes a long way, and it can be bought here in little thimbles. In some parts of Italy it is added to fish soups and it colours and flavours the well known Milanese Risotto (see page 65).

Wines

When you serve an Italian meal, you will naturally wish to serve an Italian wine with it. Grapes grow everywhere, although oddly enough, the visitor may see little evidence of them. The Italians grow vines – just anywhere – as the Englishman might grow cabbages.

In the Autumn grape harvest, donkeys and mules can be seen in the country districts with huge panniers straddled across their backs, struggling up the steep slopes and cobbled roads to the wine presses.

Chianti is one of the most popular wines, familiar to us all in its straw covered flask. It can be red or white and comes from Tuscany. The red Chianti goes very well with pizzas and most meat dishes.

From the province of Umbria comes *Orvieto*, a white wine which can be dry or sweet. Serve a dry Orvieto with rice and pasta dishes and with fish, and a sweet Orvieto goes well with dessert.

Another excellent white wine is *Soave* which comes from the Veneto. It is good with shell fish or rice dishes.

Asti Spumante is the famous Italian 'champagne' and *Lacrima Christi*, another sparkling wine, is made on the slopes of Vesuvius. It has a good bouquet and a unique flavour.

Marsala is the most famous of Italian dessert wines. It is fortified with brandy and is used a great deal in cooking for both sweet and savoury dishes.

11

Vermouth is the favourite Italian aperitif and *Cinzano* and *Martini* are names which will be familiar to you. Vermouth, a blend of white wines, is usually made from Muscat grapes, fortified and distilled with herbs. The most popular Italian liqueurs are, perhaps, *Aurum*, which has a pleasant orange flavour and *Strega* which is flavoured with herbs and spices. *Maraschino*, made from bitter cherries, and *Ratafia*, made from almonds or black cherry kernels are used largely for flavouring fruit dishes and syrups.

Wine features considerably in Italian cookery and in some dishes it is almost indispensable. In some recipes for stews and ragouts, you will find that wine is poured over the meat after it has been browned and then allowed to reduce before stock is added. In this way, the concentrated aroma of the wine permeates the meat.

You will find the recipes which follow are all simple to make. They may not all appeal to your particular taste, but they are typically Italian and I hope you will get a great deal of pleasure in making them.

As a matter of interest, I have given the Italian name of the dish after the English translation.

Unless otherwise stated, quantities given throughout the book are for four servings.

Antipasti and Salads

Antipasti are the Italian equivalent of hors d'oeuvre or meal starters. In the truly Italian household they are served before or instead of pasta or soup.

Antipasti can be very simple – perhaps a few slices of salame or prosciutto (raw ham) with anchovies and black olives; fresh vegetables dressed with oil and lemon juice; a crisp salad or a more elaborate selection of dishes.

In the winter hot antipasti, in the form of pizzas or crostini are often served.

In Italian food shops a wide range of cured meat products can be found. These can be served alone or with other ingredients.

Prosciutto
is raw cured ham, pinkish in colour with a delicate flavour. The best comes from Parma and San Daniele. It is sliced very thinly and served with melon, fresh figs or fresh pears. You should find fresh prosciutto in Italian food shops and in some delicatessens, and it is also available in cans.

Mortadella
There are many varieties of this sausage, in different sizes and shapes. The best comes from Bologna and is a smooth textured sausage, laced with pieces of pork fat and flavoured with coriander. It can sometimes take the place of prosciutto in cooking. Other varieties may be a mixture of pork, including pig's head, and veal.

Salame

also comes in great variety, most regions making their own special kind. Salame Milano, considered one of the best, is made of equal quantities of lean pork, beef and pork fat, all finely chopped and seasoned with garlic, pepper and white wine. Genoa Salame is made with veal, pork and pork fat and is strongly flavoured. In Genoa, it is eaten with young raw broad beans and Sardo cheese.

Cotechino

is a large pork salame, weighing from 1-2 lb. but it has to be cooked. To do this, prick the skin with a fine skewer, wrap the Cotcchino in muslin (cheesecloth) and put it into a pan of cold water. Bring to the boil and simmer for 2-3 hours, according to its size. It may be served hot, cut into thick slices and accompanied by haricot beans or lentils and creamed potatoes, or left to get cold and then cut into thin slices and served as an antipasto.

You will find these sausages, and many others, in continental and delicatessen stores.

Antipasti may also consist of a wide range of ingredients arranged on a large platter lined with lettuce leaves, or served on a bed of rice. In the north of Italy, Piedmont rice is world renowned and some delicious antipasti can be prepared with rice as a basis. In the south, around Naples, pasta is used more often – the water is said to be especially suited to making it.

Here are some suggestions from which you could arrange an Antipasti Platter:

Rolls of ham; slices of Salame; black and green olives; slices of tomato; anchovies rolled round a stuffed olive or a few capers and secured with cocktail picks; strips of red or green pepper; celery cut into two-inch lengths and filled with soft cheese or liver paté; sliced hard boiled eggs; cubes of cheese, etc. Line the plate with crisp lettuce leaves and arrange the chosen ingredients in as colourful and attractive a way as possible. Although fresh anchovies are available in Italy, the Italian housewife makes much use of those canned in brine or oil for salads, stuffings and sauces. If you find the canned anchovies are too salty, soak them for an hour or so in a little milk, then pat them dry before use.

Eggs and tomatoes filled with a savoury stuffing make very appetising and attractive dishes for Antipasti. The following two recipes, served together on a platter, make a very good colour combination.

14

Tuna Stuffed Tomatoes

Pomidoro col Tonno

4 large firm tomatoes
2 hard boiled eggs
1 can tuna fish (6-7 oz.)
2 teaspoons capers
1 teaspoon chopped parsley

2-3 tablespoons ($2\frac{1}{2}$-$3\frac{3}{4}$ T)
   mayonnaise (see page 82)
pepper
4 stuffed olives

Cut each tomato in half horizontally and scoop out the seeds.
Turn them upside down to drain.
Chop the eggs very finely, add the drained and flaked tuna,
capers, parsley, mayonnaise and pepper to taste. Add a
squeeze of lemon juice if liked.
Mix all the ingredients well and pile into the tomato cases.
Garnish with half a stuffed olive.

Spinach Stuffed Eggs

Uova Sode con Spinaci

4 hard boiled eggs
2 oz. Ricotta or cream cheese
2 tablespoons ($2\frac{1}{2}$ T) cooked
   spinach, well drained and
   finely chopped

2 tablespoons ($2\frac{1}{2}$ T) grated
   Parmesan cheese
salt, pepper, nutmeg
red pepper

Cut the eggs in halves lengthways. Remove the yolks and mix
with all the other ingredients. Beat well together until smooth,
adding a little cream or top of the milk if necessary. Correct
the seasoning and pile into the egg whites.
A little red pepper can be sprinkled on top for garnish.

15

Zucchini with Walnuts

Zucchini con Noci

This can be served alone as an Antipasto or as part of an Antipasti Platter. It also makes a very good separate vegetable.

1 lb. courgettes (zucchini)
$\frac{1}{8}$ pint ($\frac{1}{4}$ cup) olive oil
4-5 spring onions (scallions), sliced
3 tablespoons ($3\frac{3}{4}$ T) dry red wine

$1\frac{1}{2}$ tablespoons ($1\frac{3}{4}$ T) lemon juice
4 tablespoons (5 T) water
6 oz. (1 cup) chopped walnuts
salt, pepper

Cut the unpeeled courgettes (zucchini) into $\frac{1}{2}$ inch slices.
Heat the oil in a pan, fry the courgettes (zucchini) and onions for 5 minutes, stirring frequently.
Add wine, lemon juice and water and simmer for 5 minutes.
Add nuts and a little seasoning as required. Leave to get cold.

Artichoke Hearts

Carciofi Sott' Olio

Fresh artichokes would be used in Italy, but for this antipasto, the canned ones are quite excellent.

1 can artichoke hearts
3 tablespoons ($3\frac{3}{4}$ T) olive oil
1 tablespoon ($1\frac{1}{4}$ T) lemon juice

1 tablespoon ($1\frac{1}{4}$ T) white wine
salt, pepper
$\frac{1}{2}$ bay leaf

Drain the artichoke hearts well. Mix all the other ingredients and pour over the artichokes.
Leave to marinate for 1-2 hours, turning occasionally so that the artichokes are well impregnated with the dressing.

French Beans

Insalata di Fagiolini

1 lb. French beans
1 clove garlic, crushed finely
3 tablespoons (3¾ T) olive oil

1 tablespoon (1¼ T) lemon
  juice
salt, black pepper

Prepare the beans, stringing if necessary, and cook them in boiling salted water until just tender. Be careful not to over cook. Drain well, cut into pieces and chill.
Mix the rest of the ingredients for the dressing. Toss the beans in the dressing just before serving.

Mushrooms in Marinade

Funghi Marinati

6 peppercorns
1 bay leaf
½ teaspoon salt
1 lb. small mushrooms

¼ pint (½ cup) olive oil
juice of 2 lemons
6 tablespoons (7½ T) water
2 cloves garlic, crushed

Put the oil, lemon juice, water, garlic, peppercorns, bay leaf and salt into a pan and bring slowly to boiling point.
Strain and return the marinade to the pan. Bring to boiling point.
Wipe or peel the mushrooms as necessary. Put into the marinade and simmer for 5 minutes. Leave to get cold in the marinade.
Drain carefully and arrange in a bowl, or on a platter, as one ingredient of an Antipasti.

Hot Antipasti

These can be very pleasant to serve in the cold weather and are generally quite small and simple, consisting of crostini, which are rounds of bread, fried or baked, with a topping of cheese, shellfish, anchovies etc. They could also be individual pizzas or fritters of some kind.

Cheese and Anchovy Sandwiches

Crostini di Mozzarella con Acciughe

4 slices white bread
8 anchovy fillets
4 thin slices Mozzarella cheese
pepper
oil or butter for frying

Remove the crusts from the bread and cut each slice in half. Put a slice of cheese on one half, sprinkle with pepper and criss-cross with the anchovy fillets. Press the other half slice of bread on top.
Heat the oil in a pan and fry the sandwiches until brown on one side and the cheese has melted, then turn and brown the other side. Avoid turning the crostini before the cheese has melted or the two pieces of bread will not stick together.

Cheese and Anchovy Savouries

Crostini alla Napoletana

4 slices bread, cut about
$\frac{1}{4}$ inch thick
oil
4 oz. Bel Paese or processed
cheese
6 anchovy fillets

2 firm tomatoes, peeled and
sliced
pepper
pinch of dried basil
pinch of dried oregano or
marjoram

Cut each slice of bread in half cornerways and place on an
oiled baking sheet.
Put a thin slice of cheese on each piece of bread, criss-cross
with strips of anchovy and top with slices of tomato.
Sprinkle with pepper and herbs and dribble 1 teaspoon oil
over each.
Bake in a moderate oven (350°F., Gas Mark 4) for
about 15 minutes or until the bread is crisp and the cheese has
melted.

Chicken Livers on Toast

Crostini alla Fiorentina

$\frac{1}{2}$ lb. chicken livers
2 tablespoons ($2\frac{1}{2}$ T) oil
2 tablespoons ($2\frac{1}{2}$ T) finely
chopped onion

2-3 fresh sage leaves
freshly ground black pepper
4 slices lightly toasted bread

Wash the livers, remove any tissue and pat dry. Chop very
finely.
Heat the oil and sauté the onion and sage leaves until the
onion is soft and beginning to colour. Remove sage.
Put the chopped livers into the pan, season with pepper and
cook over low heat until the livers are cooked and no pink
colour remains.
Spread the mixture on the toast and serve at once.

Anchovies on Toast

Crostini Di Acciughe

If you do not like too strong an anchovy flavour, soak the anchovies for about 1 hour in a little milk, then pat dry before using.

1 small can (about 2 oz.) anchovy fillets

1 tablespoon ($1\frac{1}{4}$ T) finely grated onion

2 tablespoons ($2\frac{1}{2}$ T) chopped parsley

1 tablespoon ($1\frac{1}{4}$ T) olive oil

1 tablespoon ($1\frac{1}{4}$ T) lemon juice

4 slices hot toast

Chop the anchovies finely. Add the onion, parsley, oil and lemon juice and beat well with a wooden spoon until the mixture is soft and spreadable.

Spread on the hot toast and put under a hot grill (broiler) for about 2 minutes.

Cut into fingers and serve at once.

Potato and Tuna Salad

Insalata di Patate e Tonna

4 medium size potatoes

salt, pepper

1 medium size onion, peeled and sliced thinly

4 tablespoons (5 T) olive oil

1 teaspoon wine vinegar

1 can tuna fish (6-7 oz.)

1 tablespoon ($1\frac{1}{4}$ T) chopped parsley

capers

Boil the potatoes in their skins, peel and slice while warm and season with salt and pepper.

Mix in the onion, add the oil and vinegar and stir in lightly.

Leave until about 1 hour before serving, then add the tuna, drained and broken up into pieces.

Sprinkle with parsley and capers.

Rice and Scampi Salad

Insalata de Riso e Scampi

6 oz. ¾ cup) Italian rice (see
   page 62)
salt, pepper
nutmeg
4 tablespoons (5 T) olive oil
1 tablespoon (1¼ T) lemon
   juice
2-3 thin slices onion, shredded
½ red pepper, seeded and cut
   into thin strips

3 oz. (1 cup) cooked green
   peas
1 tablespoon (1¼ T) chopped
   parsley
few black olives
12 large scampi or prawns
   (shrimps)

Cook the rice in salted boiling water until just tender. Drain,
add a little salt and pepper and a grating of nutmeg.
Blend the oil and lemon juice and stir lightly into the rice.
Leave to get cold, then add all the other ingredients.

Ham and Pasta Salad

Insalata di Prosciutto e Pasta

4 oz. (1 cup) medium pasta
   shells
½ lb. Prosciutto or cooked
   ham, cut into dice
6 oz. Bel Paese cheese, cut
   into dice
2-3 stalks celery, chopped

3-4 spring onions (scallions)
   chopped
2 teaspoons prepared mustard
¼ pint (½ cup) mayonnaise
   (see page   )
lettuce, hard boiled egg,
   tomato for garnish

Cook the shell pasta in plenty of salted, boiling water for 11
minutes, then drain well and leave to get cold.
Put the ham, cheese, celery and onions into a bowl and mix
well. Add the cold pasta and mix lightly with the other
ingredients.
Stir the mustard into the mayonnaise, pour over the pasta
mixture and toss all lightly together.
Serve on a bed of lettuce and garnish with hard boiled egg
and tomato.

Macaroni Salad

Insalata Maccheroni

This makes an attractive filling for a jellied tomato or spinach ring.

4 oz. (1 cup) elbow macaroni
1½ tablespoons (1⅝ T) lemon
 juice
2 tablespoons (2½ T) vinegar
1 tablespoon (1¼ T) olive oil
2 tablespoons (2½ T) chopped
 chives or 1 teaspoon grated
 onion
3-4 stalks celery (with leaves
 if possible), diced

3 tablespoons (3¾ T) chopped
 parsley
2 tablespoons (2½ T) chopped
 canned pimento
12 stuffed olives, chopped
3 tablespoons (3¾ T) sour
 cream
1-2 tomatoes for garnish
salt, pepper
lettuce or escarole

Cook the macaroni in plenty of salted boiling water until just
tender – 'al dente'.
Mix the lemon juice, oil and vinegar well together.
When the macaroni is cooked, drain it well and while still hot,
toss in the dressing, then set aside to cool.
Mix all the other ingredients, season with salt and freshly
ground pepper.
When ready to serve, mix with the macaroni and arrange on a
bed of lettuce or escarole.
Garnish with slices or wedges of tomato.

MACARONI SALAD IN TOMATO RING. HAM AND PASTA SALAD. PASTA AND
CHICKEN SALAD (*Photograph: Pasta Foods Limited*)

Pasta and Chicken Salad

Insalata di Pasta e Pollo

4 oz. (1 cup) pasta, small
  shells or rings
4 tablespoons (5 T) olive oil
$1\frac{1}{2}$ tablespoons ($1\frac{3}{4}$ T) lemon
  juice
grated nutmeg
$\frac{1}{2}$ lb. ($1\frac{3}{4}$ cups) cooked diced
  chicken

4 oz. ($1\frac{1}{2}$ cups) cooked peas
1 red pepper, seeded and cut
  into shreds
1-2 stalks celery, sliced
  diagonally
lettuce or escarole
salt, pepper

Cook the pasta in plenty of salted, boiling water for about 12
minutes, then drain well and while still hot, add the mixed
oil and lemon juice and toss well together. Set aside to chill.
When ready to serve, add seasoning, a pinch of nutmeg,
chicken, peas, red pepper and celery.
Arrange some leaves of lettuce round a salad bowl and pile the
mixture in the centre.

Olive Salad

Olive Insalata

$\frac{1}{2}$ lb. pitted green olives
$\frac{1}{2}$ lb. pitted black olives
3 stalks celery, chopped
1 green pepper, seeded and
  cut into thin strips

1 red pepper, seeded and
  cut into thin strips
$\frac{1}{8}$ teaspoon oregano
4 tablespoons (5 T) olive oil
salt, pepper

Mix all ingredients together and refrigerate for at least 1 hour
before serving.
If there is any of this salad left, it will keep for several days in
the refrigerator.

Mushroom and Prawn (Shrimp) Salad

$\frac{1}{2}$ lb. button mushrooms
4 tablespoons (5 T) olive oil
1 tablespoon ($1\frac{1}{4}$ T) lemon
   juice

black pepper
lettuce
$\frac{1}{2}$ lb. large prawns, (shrimps),
   cooked and shelled

Wipe and slice the mushrooms.
Mix oil, lemon juice and a little pepper and pour over the mushrooms. Leave for at least 1 hour.
Line a bowl or platter with lettuce leaves. Mix mushrooms and prawns (shrimps) and arrange on lettuce.

Tomato and Scampi Salad

Insalata di Pomidori e Scampi

4 large firm tomatoes
3-4 tablespoons ($3\frac{3}{4}$-5 T)
   cooked rice
2 tablespoons ($2\frac{1}{2}$ T) chopped
   capers
2-3 gherkins, chopped
1 tablespoon ($1\frac{1}{4}$ T) chopped
   parsley

$\frac{1}{2}$ small red or green pepper,
   chopped
scampi – fresh, canned or
   frozen
mayonnaise (see page 82)
salt, pepper
4 large black olives
lettuce

Cut a slice from the top of the tomatoes and carefully remove the pulp. Discard the seeds and put the flesh into a bowl.
Add the rice, capers, gherkins, parsley, chopped green pepper and scampi, reserving a few for garnish.
Bind all the ingredients together with mayonnaise and correct the seasoning.
Fill the tomato cases, cover with a little more mayonnaise and garnish with a black olive and the remaining scampi.
Serve on a bed of lettuce.

Scampi, Apple and Cheese Salad

Insalata di Scampi, Mela e Formaggio

This makes a very attractive and delicious salad. It can be served as a first course or as a separate salad.

$\frac{1}{2}$ lb. Ricotto or cottage cheese
3 oz. ($\frac{1}{2}$ cup) chopped toasted nuts
escarole, Batavian endive or lettuce
1 dessert apple, cored, sliced
   and brushed with lemon
   juice
12-16 fresh or frozen scampi
   or prawns (shrimps)

Dressing
3 tablespoons ($3\frac{3}{4}$ T) oil
1 tablespoon ($1\frac{1}{4}$ T) lemon
   juice
salt, black pepper
$\frac{1}{2}$ avocado pear, mashed
1 tablespoon ($1\frac{1}{4}$ T) cream

Roll the cheese into balls about the size of a walnut, (if cottage cheese is used, it should be sieved) then roll in the chopped nuts. Chill while assembling the other ingredients.

Put some shredded escarole or other salad plant into 4 glasses or individual salad dishes and arrange the cheese balls, apple slices and scampi on top.

Combine the olive oil and lemon juice for the dressing, add a little salt and black pepper, the mashed avocado pear and cream. Mix all the ingredients well and pour a little over each salad just before serving.

Aubergine Salad

Insalata Caponatina

This is an antipasto from Sicily. It can also be served as a vegetable course. Sometimes anchovies are included in the mixture.

3 tablespoons ($3\frac{3}{4}$ T) oil
1 tablespoon ($1\frac{1}{4}$ T) butter
1 small onion, peeled and
   sliced
1 clove garlic, chopped

2 large aubergines (egg plants),
   finely sliced
1 × 8 oz. can (1 cup) Italian
   tomatoes
1 small head celery, chopped

SCAMPI, APPLE AND CHEESE SALAD (*Photograph: The Fruit Producers' Council*)

2 tablespoons (2½ T) black
   olives, pitted and chopped
1 tablespoon (1¼ T) capers
1 tablespoon (1¼ T) sugar

2 tablespoons (2½ T) white
   vinegar
salt, pepper

Heat the oil and butter in a pan, fry onion and garlic until the
onion begins to soften. Add aubergines, finely sliced and fry
until they begin to brown.
Add tomatoes, celery, olives and capers. Cover, and cook over
gentle heat until the vegetables are tender.
Dissolve the sugar in the vinegar and stir into the vegetables.
Cook for 15 minutes over low heat, stirring frequently.
Correct the seasoning, then leave to get quite cold before
serving.

Rice Salad

Insalata di Riso

6 oz. (¾ cup) Italian rice (see page 62)
4 tablespoons (5 T) olive oil
1 tablespoon (1¼ T) tarragon
   vinegar
salt, pepper
1 small red pepper, seeded
   and cut into thin strips
2 tablespoons (2½ T) pine nuts
   or shredded almonds
½ root fennel, shredded finely
2 tablespoons (2½ T) seedless
   raisins

3 oz. (1 cup) cooked
   green peas
4 oz. (½ cup) diced
   cooked ham
1 tablespoon (1¼ T)
   chopped parsley
½ teaspoon oregano or
   marjoram
lettuce

Cook the rice in salted boiling water until only just tender.
Drain well.
Mix the oil, vinegar, little salt and pepper, pour over the rice
and toss lightly.
Add all the other ingredients and toss lightly but well together.
Leave in a cold place for at least 1 hour, then serve on a bed of
lettuce.

Zucchini Salad

Insalata di Zucchini

Allow 2 courgettes (zucchini) about 4-5 inches long for each person
1 onion, peeled and very finely chopped
1 clove garlic, very finely crushed
2 tablespoons (2½ T) lemon juice
salt, black pepper
6 tablespoons (7½ T) olive oil

4 tomatoes, peeled, seeded and chopped
½ small green pepper, chopped finely
1 tablespoon (1¼ T) capers, chopped
1 teaspoon finely chopped parsley
1 teaspoon finely chopped basil
lettuce

Put the unpeeled courgettes (zucchini) into salted boiling water and simmer for 6-7 minutes. Drain, cut in halves, scoop out the seeds and place, cut side uppermost, onto a flat dish.
Sprinkle with half the chopped onion and garlic.
Make a dressing with the lemon juice, salt, pepper and oil and pour half over the courgettes (zucchini). Cover with foil and leave in the refrigerator to marinate for about 4 hours.
When ready for use, drain off the marinade and discard the onion and garlic.
Mix the tomatoes, green pepper, capers, parsley, basil and remaining chopped onion with the remaining dressing, add salt and black pepper to taste and fill the courgette (zucchini) cases with the mixture.
Arrange on lettuce leaves.

Soups

Soups are an important part of the Italian menu. Each province, town and even village seems to have its own speciality or some characteristic accompaniment.

Thick soups are really thick, containing a variety of vegetables and rice or pasta in addition. Minestrone is an example of this type.

The Italians also make a variety of broths and consommés, sometimes served alone, with perhaps some small pasta or rice added or as a basis for other soups. Then there are also vegetable purées and cream soups. Fish soups or stews, which are almost a meal in themselves, will be found in the section on Fish.

In many soups lavish use is made of grated Parmesan cheese, either stirred into the soup, or served separately.

In Genoa, in addition to adding grated cheese, a little Pesto, (see page 85) is added to Minestrone. Around Rome one often finds soups flavoured with the mint which grows wild there. Another characteristic touch is the crostini, (see page 19) served in place of croutons. These are small rounds of bread, spread with cheese and browned under the grill (broiler) or heated in the oven just long enough to crisp the bread and melt the cheese.

A clear consommé may be served before a dish of pasta or rice but the more substantial soups are served in place of pasta. The Italian housewife will often serve a good sustaining minestrone type of soup for supper, followed by fruit and cheese.

A good chicken or beef broth forms the basis of many Italian soups, but for the busy housewife, a good canned consommé or beef or chicken bouillon cubes will give a good result.

The three following recipes are examples of clear soups to which eggs are added in one form or another. They are simple to make, and are delicious and sustaining.

Pavia Soup

Zuppa Pavese

*This soup is popular all over Italy and contains all the ingredients for a ligh(
meal – consommé, egg, bread and cheese.*

4 eggs	12 small rounds bread
1½-2 pints (3¾-5 cups) good	butter
chicken or beef consommé	grated Parmesan cheese

Fry the rounds of bread in butter until lightly browned on
both sides. Sprinkle with cheese and keep warm.
Heat the consommé in a shallow pan. Break the eggs, one at a
time into a saucer and slide carefully into the hot consommé.
As each egg is poached, use a slotted spoon and remove it
carefully to a soup plate. Strain some of the hot consommé
over the egg and arrange three of the rounds of bread around
each.

Ragged Egg Soup

Stracciatella

*This soup is so named because of its appearance. The egg mixture is
stirred into very hot chicken bouillon and it breaks up into little threads
or flakes.*

2 eggs	Parmesan cheese
2 tablespoons (2½ T) fine	2 pints (5 cups) chicken
semolina	bouillon
4 tablespoons (5 T) grated	parsley

Beat the eggs, semolina and cheese together.
Add about ¼ pint (½ cup) of the bouillon and stir to a smooth
cream. Heat the rest of the bouillon until it is almost boiling.
Add the egg mixture and stir vigorously with a fork for 3-4
minutes.
Allow the soup to come just below boiling point, then pour
into a hot tureen, sprinkle with parsley and serve at once.

Paradise Soup

Zuppa Paradiso

2 eggs
2 tablespoons (2½ T) grated
  Parmesan cheese
2 tablespoons (2½ T)
  breadcrumbs

2 pints (5 cups) chicken or
  beef consommé
freshly ground white pepper,
  salt, nutmeg

Separate the eggs and beat the whites until stiff, then beat in
the yolks.
Add cheese, breadcrumbs, seasoning and nutmeg to taste.
Heat the consommé to boiling point, then gradually add the
egg mixture a spoonful at a time.
Cook for 6-7 minutes and serve.

Chestnut Soup

Zuppa di Castagne

¾ lb. chestnuts
2 oz. (¼ cup) bacon fat or butter
2 onions, peeled and chopped
1 carrot, peeled and chopped
1-2 stalks celery, chopped

2½ pints (6 cups) stock or
  water
salt, pepper
nutmeg
slices of fried bread

Score the chestnuts once or twice on the rounded side, put on
to a baking tray and put into a slow oven, 300°F, Gas Mark 2,
for about 10 minutes.
Remove the outer and inner skins.
Heat the bacon fat in a saucepan, add the vegetables and fry
until the onion is golden brown. Add chestnuts and stock and
cook until the chestnuts are tender.
Rub through a sieve.
Return to the pan and season carefully. The amount of salt and
pepper required will depend on the stock used. Add a pinch of
nutmeg and re-heat the soup.
Serve with slices of fried bread.
A can of unsweetened chestnut purée could be used to make
this soup.

Chicken Cream Soup

Zuppa Crema de Pollo

2 tablespoons (2½ T) ground
  rice
¼ pint (½ cup) milk
2½ pints (6 cups) chicken
  consommé
lemon juice

nutmeg, pepper, salt
2 eggs
2 tablespoons (2½ T) cream
2 tablespoons (2½ T) chopped
  parsley

Mix the ground rice smoothly with the milk.
Heat the consommé, add the rice mixture, stir until boiling
then simmer for about 20 minutes.
Season carefully with lemon juice, nutmeg and pepper to taste.
A little salt may be required, but this depends on the basic
consommé. Strain the soup and return to the pan to heat.
Beat the eggs, add a little of the hot soup, then add the egg
mixture gradually to the hot soup. Be sure the soup does *not*
boil. Just before serving, stir in the cream and parsley.

Consommé with Pasta and Chicken Livers

Pasta in Brodo con Fegatini

3 oz. small pasta – shells, stars
  or alphabet egg pasta
12 oz. fresh green peas,
  weighed after shelling
2 pints (5 cups) chicken
  bouillon

3-4 oz. chicken livers
butter
salt, pepper
chopped parsley
grated Parmesan cheese

Cook the pasta and peas in salted, boiling water for about 5
minutes, then drain well. Heat the bouillon, add the pasta
and peas and cook gently until the rice is tender.
Meanwhile, clean and chop the chicken livers and cook for a
few minutes in a little butter.
When the rice is cooked, add the livers and any butter
remaining in the pan. Correct the seasoning and serve sprinkled
with chopped parsley and grated Parmesan cheese.

Green Soup

Zuppa di Verdura

2 tablespoons (2½ T) oil
4-5 leeks, chopped coarsely
1½ lb. spinach, chopped
½ lettuce, shredded
1 tablespoon (1¼ T) chopped
   mint

2 pints (5 cups) chicken
   bouillon
1 lb. green peas, weighed
   after shelling
salt, pepper, nutmeg
chopped parsley

Heat the oil in a pan, add leeks and cook until softening.
Add spinach, lettuce and mint and stir over low heat for 2-3
minutes. Add the hot bouillon and peas, bring to boiling point,
cover and simmer until the vegetables are tender.
Pass through a sieve or vegetable mill, add salt and pepper to
taste and a pinch of nutmeg.
Reheat, and serve sprinkled with parsley.
This soup should be quite thick, but it can be diluted with a
little stock if necessary.

Rice and Green Pea Soup

Risi e Bisi

1 tablespoon (1¼ T) oil
1 tablespoon (1¼ T) butter
1 onion, peeled and chopped
¾ lb. (1½ cups) Italian rice
1½ lb. green peas, weighed
   after shelling

2 pints (5 cups) chicken stock
salt, pepper
1 teaspoon finely chopped
   mint
grated Parmesan cheese

Heat the oil and butter in a pan. Add the onion and fry until
soft and transparent.
Add the rice, stir over low heat for about 5 minutes, then add
the peas and cook a further 2-3 minutes until the ingredients
are well impregnated with the fat.
Add the hot stock, bring to boiling point, then cover and
simmer until the rice is tender – about 15-20 minutes.
Add salt and pepper to taste and the mint.
Serve with grated Parmesan cheese.

Minestrone

This should be a thick colourful soup and you can use your imagination and ingenuity as far as the recipe is concerned. Almost any vegetable can be used according to the season. You will need herbs, some small pasta or rice, or both and, of course, some grated Parmesan cheese. Obviously, some vegetables take longer to cook than others, so bear this in mind when making the soup. It is not a soup to choose to make when you are in a hurry and it is worth while making a fairly large quantity at one time. The following recipe will give you an idea of the general method, but it can be varied as you wish.

$\frac{1}{4}$ lb. small white haricot (navy) beans
3 tablespoons ($3\frac{3}{4}$ T) oil
2 onions, peeled and sliced
2 cloves garlic, crushed
2-3 rashers (slices) bacon
4 tomatoes, peeled, seeded and chopped
1 small glass red wine
1 teaspoon marjoram, chopped
$\frac{1}{2}$ teaspoon thyme, chopped
2 carrots, peeled and cut into cubes

2 potatoes, peeled and cut into cubes
1 small turnip, peeled and cubed
1-2 stalks celery, chopped
$\frac{1}{2}$ small cabbage, shredded
2 oz. ($\frac{1}{2}$ cup) macaroni or small pasta – little shells, stars etc.
1 tablespoon ($1\frac{1}{4}$ T) chopped parsley
salt, pepper
grated Parmesan cheese

Soak the beans overnight.
Heat the oil in a large saucepan, add the onion, garlic and bacon and sauté for a few minutes. Add tomatoes, wine and haricot beans. Add 3 pints water ($7\frac{1}{2}$ cups), marjoram and thyme and simmer for about 2 hours, covered.
Add carrots, cook about 10 minutes, then add potatoes and turnips. Cook a few minutes longer, then add celery, cabbage and pasta. Cook until pasta and all vegetables are tender, then add chopped parsley, salt and pepper to taste and stir in 2-3 tablespoons ($2\frac{1}{2}$-$3\frac{3}{4}$ T) grated Parmesan. Serve with extra Parmesan.

Milan Minestrone

Minestrone Genovese

This is a variation of the preceding recipe. The haricot beans are omitted and rice is used instead of pasta.

1 tablespoon (1¼ T) oil
1 onion, peeled and chopped
1 clove garlic, crushed
2 carrots, peeled and chopped
2 stalks celery, chopped
4 oz. (½ cup) diced green bacon
2 pints (5 cups) stock or water
1 large potato, peeled and diced
¼ small cabbage, shredded
1 courgette (zucchini) chopped

2 oz. (½ cup) shelled green peas
1 tablespoon (1¼ T) tomato purée
4 oz. (½ cup) Italian rice
1 tablespoon (1¼ T) chopped parsley
1 teaspoon chopped sage
1 teaspoon chopped oregano
grated Parmesan cheese
salt, pepper

Heat the oil in a large saucepan. (The bacon will give the necessary extra fat.)
Add onion, garlic, carrots, celery and bacon and cook until the onion is soft and transparent.
Add stock, remaining vegetables and tomato puree, cover and cook over low heat for about 40 minutes.
Add rice, parsley and sage and continue to cook a further 15-20 minutes. Add salt and pepper to taste and serve with grated Parmesan cheese.

Vegetables

There is a wide variety of vegetables available in Italy. They are generally served as a separate course, before or after the meat or as a first course, as you will have seen in the first section of this book.

Italian housewives go to a great deal of trouble in selecting their vegetables and cook them with imagination and care. Vegetables such as aubergines (egg plants), courgettes (zucchini), globe artichokes, peppers and tomatoes are frequently stuffed and you will find examples of these in the recipes which follow. Fennel is used a great deal, both uncooked, either as a salad or at the end of the meal with fruit and cooked when, like zucchini, it is delicious coated with a light batter (see recipe for Pastella on page 89) and fried in oil.

Cabbage, that most mundane of vegetables, is transformed into an elegant dish by the Italian housewife who serves it with a sweet-sour sauce or stuffs the leaves with a savoury filling.

Stuffed Artichokes

Carciofi Ripieni

4 globe artichokes
2 tablespoons (2½ T) butter
½ small onion, peeled and finely chopped
1 clove garlic, crushed
3-4 mushrooms, sliced
a few small flowerets cauliflower
2 tablespoons (2½ T) breadcrumbs
1 tablespoon (1¼ T) chopped parsley
olive oil
6 tablespoons (7½ T) dry white wine
salt, pepper

Remove the stalks and any coarse outside leaves from the
artichokes and cut off about 1 inch from the top of the leaves.
Pull the artichokes apart carefully and remove the choke.
Heat the butter in a pan, add the onion, garlic, mushrooms and
cauliflower and sauté for 5 minutes, then stir in breadcrumbs
and parsley. Season to taste and stuff the artichokes.
Heat a little oil in a pan large enough to take the four
artichokes. Put them in the pan and add the wine. Cover, and
simmer over very low heat for about 1 hour.

Stuffed Green Peppers

Peperoni Ripieni

4 even sized green peppers
$\frac{1}{4}$ pint ($\frac{1}{2}$ cup) olive oil
1 small onion, peeled and
　finely chopped
6 oz. ($\frac{3}{4}$ cup) diced bacon

1 × 8 oz. can peeled Italian
　tomatoes
salt, pepper
6 oz. (2 cups) cooked rice

Cut a slice from the stalk end of the peppers and remove seeds
and pith. Blanch in boiling water for 5 minutes, drain well.
Heat about 2 tablespoons ($2\frac{1}{2}$ T) of the oil in a pan, add onion,
and fry until soft and transparent. Add bacon, fry for a few
minutes, then add contents of the can of tomatoes, salt and
pepper. Simmer for 3-4 minutes. Add rice, and stir until the
liquid has been absorbed. Correct the seasoning.
Arrange the peppers in a deep casserole and fill with the rice
mixture. Pour over the rest of the oil.
Cover, and cook in a moderate oven, 350°F., Gas Mark 4 for
about 40 minutes.

Herb Stuffed Mushrooms

Funghi Ripieni

Choose rather large, cup shaped mushrooms for this dish. They can be served as a separate course at the beginning or end of a meal, or as an accompaniment to other dishes.

1 lb. mushrooms
2 oz. ($\frac{1}{4}$ cup) chopped cooked ham
1 teaspoon finely chopped
   oregano
$\frac{1}{4}$ teaspoon chopped thyme
1 teaspoon chopped parsley

2 tablespoons ($2\frac{1}{2}$ T) grated
   Parmesan cheese
2 tablespoons ($2\frac{1}{2}$ T)
   breadcrumbs
olive oil
salt, pepper

Wash the mushrooms, remove the stalks, trim as necessary and then chop them finely.

Mix the chopped mushroom stalks with the ham, herbs, grated cheese and breadcrumbs. Season to taste.

Put the mushrooms into a fireproof dish and fill with the mixture. Pour a little oil on each mushroom, cover, and cook in a moderate oven, 350°F., Gas Mark 4 for about 20-25 minutes.

Add a little extra oil if necessary while the mushrooms are cooking so that they do not become dry.

Aubergines with Cheese and Tomatoes

Parmigiana

This is a popular dish in and around Naples.

about 2 lb. aubergines (egg
   plant)
salt
flour
olive oil

$\frac{1}{2}$ lb. Mozzarella cheese
2 oz. ($\frac{1}{2}$ cup) grated Parmesan
   cheese
$\frac{1}{4}$ pint ($\frac{1}{2}$ cup) tomato sauce,
   (see page 84)

HERB-STUFFED MUSHROOMS (*Photograph: Angel Studio*)

Peel the aubergines, cut into slices lengthways and put into a colander. Sprinkle with salt and leave to drain for about 1 hour or longer.

Sprinkle lightly with flour and fry in a little olive oil. Drain on soft paper.

Put about 1 tablespoon (1¼ T) oil into a fireproof dish or casserole. Put in a layer of the fried aubergines, cover with a thin layer of Mozzarella cheese and then a little sauce.

Continue in layers until all the ingredients are used up.

Cover with grated Parmesan, sprinkle with oil and cook in a moderate oven, 350°F., Gas Mark 4 for about 20-30 minutes.

Cabbage with Bacon and Fennel

Cavolo Agra

1 small firm cabbage
3 rashers (slices) bacon, chopped
1 pint (2½ cups) water

1 tablespoon (1¼ T) white wine vinegar
pepper, salt
1 teaspoon fennel seeds

Wash, drain and shred the cabbage.

Heat a pan large enough to take all the cabbage, put in the bacon and fry until the fat begins to run.

Add the shredded cabbage, water, vinegar, seasoning and fennel seeds. Cook, uncovered, over low heat until the cabbage is tender and most of the liquid evaporated.

If fennel seeds are not available, use caraway seeds instead.

Red Peppers

Peperonata

This colourful dish makes a good accompaniment to boiled chicken or it can be served as an antipasto, as it is equally good cold. Peperonata re-heats very successfully.

4 red peppers
3 tablespoons ($3\frac{3}{4}$ T) olive oil
1 tablespoon ($1\frac{1}{4}$ T) butter
1 small onion, peeled and very finely chopped

$\frac{1}{2}$ clove garlic, crushed
4-5 ripe tomatoes, peeled, seeded and quartered
salt, pepper
chopped parsley

Wash and dry the peppers, cut in half lengthways, remove seeds and pith and cut into strips.
Heat the oil and butter in a pan, add the onion and garlic and cook until the onion is soft and transparent.
Add the peppers and a little salt, cover, and sauté in the oil for about 15 minutes.
Add tomatoes and cook over low heat for about 30 minutes, stirring occasionally, until the mixture is fairly thick and dry.
Sprinkle with chopped parsley before serving.

Tomatoes with Olives

Pomidoro con Olive

4 large tomatoes
3 tablespoons ($3\frac{3}{4}$ T) green olives, chopped
6 oz. ($\frac{3}{4}$ cup) minced (ground) cooked ham

3 tablespoons ($3\frac{3}{4}$ T) finely chopped parsley
$\frac{1}{2}$ teaspoon chopped basil
mayonnaise

Cut tomatoes in halves crossways and place cut side up in a buttered baking dish. Cook in a moderate oven 350 !F., Gas Mark 4 for about 7-10 minutes. Be careful not to overcook.
Mix olives, ham, parsley and basil and add just enough mayonnaise to bind.
Spoon on top of the tomatoes and put under a hot grill (broiler) for a few minutes to brown lightly.

Stuffed Zucchini

Zucchini Ripieni

1 large slice bread
milk
1 lb. courgettes (zucchini)
4 mushrooms, chopped
2 anchovy fillets, chopped
2 rashers (slices) bacon,
    chopped
3 tablespoons ($3\frac{3}{4}$ T) grated
    Parmesan cheese

1 teaspoon chopped fresh
    basil, marjoram or parsley
black pepper
1 egg yolk
2 teaspoons breadcrumbs
oil

Remove the crusts from the bread and soak for 5-10 minutes in a little milk, then squeeze dry.

Put the unpeeled courgettes (zucchini) into salted, boiling water for 3 minutes. Drain well, cut in halves lengthways and scoop out the flesh with a teaspoon.

Put the mushrooms, anchovy fillets, bacon, 2 tablespoons ($2\frac{1}{2}$ T) of the cheese, basil, soaked bread and courgette (zucchini) flesh in a bowl. Add a little black pepper and mix well together. Bind with the egg yolk.

Fill the zucchini halves with this mixture and arrange in a lightly oiled fireproof dish.

Mix the remaining cheese and breadcrumbs together and sprinkle over the top. Sprinkle with oil and bake in a moderate oven 350°F., Gas Mark 4 for about 35-40 minutes.

Zucchini with Ham

Zucchini alla Romano

1 lb. courgettes (zucchini)
flour
salt, pepper
oil
2 onions, peeled and chopped

1 clove garlic, crushed
$\frac{1}{2}$ lb. ham, cut into 4 pieces
2 oz. ($\frac{1}{2}$ cup) grated Parmesan
    cheese

Cut the courgettes (zucchini) into fairly thick slices and coat with flour to which a little salt and pepper has been added. Heat a little oil in a pan, add the onion and garlic and cook until the onion is soft and translucent.

Add the pieces of ham and brown lightly. Remove the ham and onion on to a plate. Heat a little more oil in the pan, put in the slices of courgettes (zucchini) and leave just long enough to brown lightly.

Arrange most of the slices of courgettes (zucchini) in a buttered fireproof dish, sprinkle with half the onion and half the grated cheese. Put the ham on top, sprinkle with the remaining onion and cheese and top with the rest of the zucchini.

Put into a moderate oven, 375°F., Gas Mark 5 for about 15 minutes.

Beans with Sweet Peppers

Fagiolini con Peperoni

1 lb. French beans
4 rashers (slices) bacon
3 tablespoons ($3\frac{3}{4}$ T) diced
   green or red peppers

3 tablespoons ($3\frac{3}{4}$ T) red wine
   vinegar
$\frac{1}{2}$ teaspoon sugar
$\frac{1}{4}$ teaspoon dry mustard
Tabasco sauce

Prepare the beans and cook whole in salted, boiling water. Drain well.

Cut the bacon into strips and fry until crisp, drain from the fat and put with the beans.

Add diced peppers, vinegar, sugar and mustard to the fat left in the pan and stir until boiling.

Add a few drops of Tabasco, pour over the beans and bacon and mix well.

Fried Zucchini

Zucchini Fritti

This is a very simple recipe but it is included because the courgettes (zucchini) cooked this way are so delicious.

Cut the unpeeled courgettes (zucchini) into small strips. Put them into a colander, sprinkle with salt and leave for about an hour to drain. Shake them in a cloth with flour and a little salt, then fry for about 3 minutes in deep oil.
Drain well on soft paper and serve at once.

Stuffed Aubergines

Melanzane Ripiene

3 large even sized aubergines (egg plants)
6 tablespoons ($7\frac{1}{2}$ T) breadcrumbs
2 tablespoons ($2\frac{1}{2}$ T) chopped parsley
1 teaspoon chopped oregano
6 anchovy fillets
12 large black olives, pitted and chopped
3 tomatoes, peeled, seeded and chopped
3-4 tablespoons ($3\frac{3}{4}$-5 T) olive oil

Cut the aubergines (egg plants) in halves lengthways, scoop out some of the flesh and put it into a bowl. Mash well with a wooden spoon.
Add breadcrumbs, parsley, oregano, finely chopped anchovy fillets, olives and tomatoes. Mix all well.
Fill the aubergines (egg plants) with the mixture, arrange in a fireproof dish and pour the oil over. Cover, and cook in a moderate oven, 350°F., Gas Mark 4 for about $\frac{3}{4}$-1 hour.

Green Peas with Ham

Piselli al Prosciutto

If you grow peas and can gather them when they are small, sweet and tender like those growing around Rome, you will enjoy this dish immensely.. Frozen peas can be used, especially the little 'petits pois', but do not attempt to use peas which have become old and wrinkled.

1 oz. (2 T) butter
1 small onion, peeled and chopped very finely
1 lb. green peas, weighed after shelling

3-4 tablespoons ($3\frac{3}{4}$-5 T) water
2-3 oz. cooked ham, cut into strips

Heat the butter in a pan over gentle heat, add the onion and cook slowly until it is soft and translucent.
Add the peas and water and cook for about 5 minutes.
Add the ham and continue to cook very gently until the peas are tender – which should not be more than 10 minutes.
If you use frozen peas, they will only take 5 minutes or less.

Baked Artichokes

Carciofi al Forno

4 globe artichokes
2 cloves garlic, crushed
2 tablespoons ($2\frac{1}{2}$ T) chopped parsley

1 oz. (2 T) butter
pepper, salt
olive oil

Wash the artichokes and cut the stalks and tips off the leaves.
Put the garlic, parsley, butter and a little salt and pepper into a mortar and pound until the mixture is smooth, then put little dabs of it between the leaves of the artichokes.
Arrange them in a fireproof dish, add $\frac{1}{2}$ pint (1 cup) hot water and sprinkle the artichokes with oil.
Cover, and cook in a moderate oven, 350°F., Gas Mark 4 for about 40 minutes, or until they are tender. (You can test by pulling out one of the leaves.) Serve with melted butter.

STUFFED AUBERGINES

Eggs with Spinach

Uova con Spinacci

2 lb. spinach
salt, pepper
$\frac{1}{4}$ teaspoon nutmeg
2 oz. ($\frac{1}{2}$ cup) grated Parmesan
   cheese

1 oz. (2 T) butter
4 eggs

Cook the spinach, drain thoroughly and chop.
Add salt, pepper, nutmeg, nearly all the cheese and butter and
mix all well together.
Divide between four individual buttered fireproof dishes and
make a well in the centre. Break an egg into each, sprinkle
with a little salt and pepper and the rest of the cheese and put
into a moderate oven, 350°F., Gas Mark 4 just long enough to
cook the eggs.

Cauliflower with Tomato and Cheese

Cavolfiore alla Romagnola

*This is a simple but delicious way of serving cauliflower as a separate
course. The walnuts could be omitted but their crunchy texture makes a
pleasant addition.*

1 cauliflower
3 tablespoons ($3\frac{3}{4}$ T) olive oil
1 tablespoon ($1\frac{1}{4}$ T) butter
1 clove garlic, crushed
2 tablespoons ($2\frac{1}{2}$ T) coarsely
   chopped walnuts
2 tablespoons ($2\frac{1}{2}$ T) chopped
   parsley

5-6 tablespoons ($6\frac{1}{4}$-$7\frac{1}{2}$ T) water
1 tablespoon ($1\frac{1}{4}$ T) tomato
   purée
salt, pepper
grated Parmesan cheese

Trim and wash the cauliflower and divide into flowerets.
Heat the oil and butter in a pan, add the garlic and walnuts
and sauté for a few minutes.

Add parsley and cauliflower, cook a few minutes then add water, tomato purée, salt and pepper. Cover, and cook over very low heat for about 25 minutes.

Turn into a serving dish and sprinkle generously with grated cheese.

Asparagus
Asparagi

In the countryside around Rome asparagus grows wild and it is delicious when cooked quite plainly and served with melted butter.

In Tuscany the spears are much larger and thicker and the Italians often serve these cold with Mayonnaise and hard boiled eggs, as shown in the picture, or with an oil and lemon juice dressing.

In the following recipe, the asparagus is cooked in the oven with cheese and tomatoes and would make an excellent light supper or luncheon dish.

Asparagus with Cheese
Asparagi alla Formaggio

1 lb. asparagus
2 oz. ($\frac{1}{4}$ cup) butter
2 tablespoons ($2\frac{1}{2}$ T) finely
   chopped onion
1-2 stalks celery, finely
   chopped
3 tablespoons ($3\frac{3}{4}$ T) grated
   Parmesan cheese

1 tablespoon ($1\frac{1}{4}$ T)
   breadcrumbs
4 tomatoes, peeled, seeded
   and diced
salt, pepper
pinch of oregano
pinch of thyme

Prepare the asparagus.

Melt the butter in a shallow baking dish and arrange the spears neatly in the bottom. Sprinkle with the onion, celery, cheese and breadcrumbs.

Add tomatoes and seasoning to taste and sprinkle with the herbs. Cover, and cook in a moderate oven, 350°F., Gas Mark 4 for about 40 minutes.

ASPARAGUS WITH MAYONNAISE AND HARD BOILED EGGS

Pasta and Rice

Pasta or rice, in some form or other, is eaten every day by most Italians. In the south of Italy it is usually a pasta dish – it is said that the water in Naples accounts for its superior brand of pasta.

In the northern provinces, Lombardy, Piedmont and the Veneto, more rice is used and the rice of Piedmont is regarded as superior to any other variety. The variety of pasta is quite astonishing and it can be all the more confusing because in different regions, almost identical pastas are known by different names.

The best pasta is made from pure durum wheat, but today, even in Italy, pasta is not always home made and it can be bought – as in England and America – in packets, mass-produced and dried.

Some pasta is made with egg, and there is the famous green pasta, flavoured and coloured with spinach.

If you look around the shelves in your local supermarket or delicatessen, you will find a big selection of pasta in different shapes and sizes. Here are just a few . . .

Spaghetti is the largest of the tubular pastas, others are vermicelli, spaghettini and fidelini which is the finest.

Flat ribbon pasta comes in different widths. Lasagne varies from $\frac{1}{2}$-2 inches and can be coloured green with spinach or pink with tomato. Fettuccine and Tagliatelle are about $\frac{1}{4}$ inch wide.

Soup pasta can be shaped like little stars, letters of the alphabet, little rings or squares.

Shaped pasta comes in the form of butterflies, bows, shells, snails etc. and then there is the pasta which is stuffed like Ravioli and Tortellini.

A dish of pasta can make a very satisfying and economical meal and there are so many ways of serving it; generally with a tomato or meat sauce, or with butter and cheese, or sprinkled with oil, as well as the more substantial additions, such as bacon, eggs, mushrooms etc.

If you are figure conscious, you can take comfort from the fact that the Italians claim if a dish of pasta is accompanied by a green salad or a dish of vegetables and followed by fruit or cheese, it will have no fattening effect.

General rules for cooking pasta

For a main dish, allow about 3 oz. pasta per person.

For use in soup, allow 4 oz. to 2 pints soup.

Remember that as a general rule, pasta will double its bulk when cooked. Cook the pasta in plenty of salted, boiling water. Twelve ounces of pasta will need about 6 pints (15 cups) of water and 1 tablespoon ($1\frac{1}{4}$ T) salt.

Be sure the water is really boiling before adding the pasta. For long spaghetti or macaroni, take the bundle in the hand and put one end in the boiling water, coiling it around inside the pan as soon as it softens. Keep the water boiling and the pan uncovered.

Do not overcook. The time depends on the type and size of the pasta and you will generally find recommended times given on the packet. The pasta should be tender but firm to bite into. This is called *al dente*. The following is just a rough guide:

Spaghetti   8–12 minutes
Thin spaghetti   6–10 minutes
Macaroni   10–12 minutes
Lasagne   6–9 minutes
Fine noodles   4–6 minutes
Alphabet pasta   5–7 minutes

When cooked, drain through a colander, put into a hot dish and add a generous lump of butter or sprinkle with a little olive oil.

Rice

As mentioned at the beginning of this section, Piedmont is the greatest rice producing area of Italy. The streams that run down the mountains are diverted to flood the rice fields, just as in the Far East.

As with most of her marketing, the Italian housewife chooses her rice with care. The best quality—a long, rather fat grain—she uses for risottos, salads and garnishes. A medium grain is good for general purposes and the small grain or 'common' rice, for soups and puddings.

You will find a selection of dishes made with rice in the following pages. In Italy rice is seldom served as a vegetable accompaniment to meat, fish or chicken, but more as a course on its own. There is, however, one exception. On page 105 you will find a recipe for Ossobuco and this is always served with Risotto Milanese.

Italian rice is now readily available in delicatessen shops and supermarkets and it is well worth using this when you are following Italian recipes. You will find the rice is often cooked slowly in stock, but as for pasta, avoid overcooking. It should be just *al dente*.

The time for cooking varies with the quality of the rice – the better the rice, the more liquid it absorbs and the longer it takes to cook.

A SELECTION OF PASTA (*Photograph: Pasta Foods Limited*)

Risotto

It is perhaps the unique cooking properties of the rice of Piedmont that have made Risotto one of the classic dishes of Northern Italy. Creamy in texture, but with every grain firm in the centre, cooked and served simply with butter and cheese, it is a delight. However, there are endless improvisations and almost anything can be added to make a more elaborate dish or, in fact, to use up a small quantity of other food such as ham, poultry, game, lobster etc.

Risotto with Ham and Peas

Risotto con Prosciutto e Piselli

2 oz. ($\frac{1}{4}$ cup) butter
1 onion, peeled and chopped
12 oz. (1$\frac{1}{2}$ cups) Italian rice
6 tablespoons (7$\frac{1}{2}$ T) dry white wine
2 pints (5 cups) chicken stock
pinch of saffron
1 small red pepper, seeded and chopped

6 oz (2 cups) cooked green peas
4 oz. ($\frac{1}{2}$ cup) cooked diced ham
salt, pepper
Parmesan cheese

Heat half the butter in a pan, add the onion and cook until it is soft and beginning to brown.
Add rice, stir until it is translucent, then add the wine and cook until it has almost evaporated.
Add half the hot stock, saffron and red pepper and cook, uncovered, until most of the stock has evaporated, then add remaining stock and continue to cook until the rice is almost ready. Stir frequently while the risotto is cooking.
Add ham and peas, season to taste and leave just long enough for the peas to heat through.
Add remaining butter and serve with a bowl of grated Parmesan cheese.

Risotto alla Milanese

There are many versions of this dish. It is always flavoured with saffron, but can be made simply with chicken stock and served with plenty of butter and grated Parmesan cheese, or with beef marrow and white wine or with Marsala.

In northern Italy, butter is always used for making risotto, whereas in the south more oil is used.

Traditionally, rice is served as a course on its own and not as a vegetable accompaniment to meat or fish dishes. There is, however, one exception, and the recipe which follows is always served with the famous Italian veal dish – Ossobucco (see page 105).

$1\frac{1}{2}$ oz. (3 T) butter

1 small onion, peeled and chopped

1 oz. beef marrow – extracted from marrow bones (but can be omitted)

12 oz. ($1\frac{1}{2}$ cups) Italian rice

$\frac{1}{2}$ pint (1 cup) white wine

about 2 pints (5 cups) hot chicken stock

$\frac{1}{2}$ teaspoon saffron

butter

grated Parmesan cheese

Heat the butter in a pan, add the onion and cook until it is soft and golden brown. Add the beef marrow and rice and stir until the rice is well impregnated with the butter.

Add the wine and cook over low heat until it is almost absorbed.

Add about $\frac{1}{2}$ pint (1 cup) hot stock, cook until it is almost absorbed and continue in this way until the stock has all been used and adding more if required. Towards the end of the cooking, stir frequently to prevent the rice from sticking. Add the saffron and butter and grated cheese to taste.

Risotto with Orange

Risotto alla Arancia

1 large orange
1 oz. (2 T) butter
1 tablespoon (1¼ T) olive oil
12 oz. (1½ cups) Italian rice
1½ pints (3¾ cups)

1 bay leaf
½ teaspoon saffron
salt, pepper
1 tablespoon (1¼ T) blanched
   shredded almonds

Cut 4-5 very thin strips of peel from the orange, using a potato
peeler. Blanch these in cold water, bring to boiling point and
discard the water. Peel the rest of the orange, removing all the
white pith and cut into segments.
Heat the butter and oil in a pan, add the rice and blanched
orange peel and stir for 1–2 minutes until the rice is
thoroughly impregnated with the butter.
Add the hot stock and bay leaf, stir well and stir in the saffron.
Cover and cook over low heat until nearly all the liquid
has been absorbed. If more convenient, the rice can be
cooked in the oven at this stage. It will take about 20 minutes.
When ready to serve, remove the bay leaf and orange peel,
add seasoning if required and stir in the orange segments and
almonds.

Risotto with Tuna

Risotto al Tonno

For the sauce
4 tablespoons (5 T) olive oil
2 tablespoons (2½ T) butter
½ Spanish onion, peeled and
   finely chopped

2 tablespoons (2½ T) tomato
   purée
6 tablespoons (7½ T) dry white
   wine
1 can, (about 7-8 oz.) tuna

Heat the oil and butter in a pan and sauté the onion until soft
and golden.
Add tomato purée, wine and flaked tuna, mix all well and
heat through, stirring all the time. Keep hot while preparing
the risotto.

For the risotto

2 oz. (4 T) butter
$\frac{1}{2}$ Spanish onion, peeled and finely chopped
12 oz. ($1\frac{1}{2}$ cups) rice
6 tablespoons ($7\frac{1}{2}$ T) dry white wine
$1\frac{1}{2}$ pints ($3\frac{3}{4}$ cups) chicken stock
grated Parmesan cheese
salt, pepper

Heat the butter in a saucepan and cook the onion in the butter until translucent. Add the rice, and cook, stirring all the time until the rice is golden.

Add wine and hot chicken stock, cover, and cook until the rice is just tender.

Stir in the tuna sauce 5 minutes before serving. Correct the seasoning, add some extra butter and a little grated cheese and serve extra cheese separately.

Risotto with Beans and Bacon

Risotto alla Paesano

4 oz. ($\frac{3}{8}$ cup) red kidney beans, soaked overnight (or use 1 small can)
2 oz. (4 T) butter
2 tablespoons ($2\frac{1}{2}$ T) oil
3 rashers (slices) bacon
1 small onion, chopped
2 small potatoes, diced
1 carrot, peeled and diced
2 courgettes (zucchini), diced
2 stalks celery, chopped
$\frac{1}{2}$ pint (1 cup) beef stock
12 oz. ($1\frac{1}{2}$ cups) rice
grated Parmesan cheese
salt, pepper

Cook the beans in salted, boiling water until tender (about 1 hour) then drain and reserve the stock.

Heat the butter and oil in the pan, add bacon and onion and cook until the onion is translucent. Add potatoes, carrot, courgette and celery and cook for 3-4 minutes, stirring.

Add beef stock and simmer, uncovered, until almost all the liquid has evaporated.

Add rice, stir over low heat for about 2 minutes, then add beans and 1 pint ($2\frac{1}{2}$ cups) of the bean stock. Cook over medium heat, adding extra stock as necessary until the rice is tender. Season and add grated cheese to taste.

Baked Lasagne

This dish is really a meal in itself. Even if you are unable to get mozzarella and ricotta cheese, the substitutes suggested will give a good lasagne. Either of the recipes for tomato sauce on page 84-5 could be used, but the following quantities will give the right amount for this special dish.

For the sauce

3 lb. ripe tomatoes, coarsely chopped

3 tablespoons ($3\frac{3}{4}$ T) tomato purée

2 carrots, peeled and roughly chopped

1 large onion, peeled and roughly chopped

2 cloves garlic, crushed

2-3 stalks celery, chopped

1 tablespoon ($1\frac{1}{4}$ T) chopped parsley

grated rind of $\frac{1}{2}$ lemon

2 tablespoons ($2\frac{1}{2}$ T) olive oil

2 tablespoons ($2\frac{1}{2}$ T) butter

$\frac{3}{4}$-1 lb. lasagne noodles

butter

$\frac{1}{2}$ lb. mozzarella or Bel Paese cheese

$\frac{1}{4}$ lb. mortadella or other Italian sausage, coarsely chopped

2 hard boiled eggs

4 oz. (1 cup) grated Parmesan cheese

8 oz. (1 cup) ricotta or cottage cheese

To make the sauce

Put the first eight ingredients into a pan, cover, and simmer for about 1 hour. Pass through a sieve, return to the pan, add seasoning to taste and continue to simmer until the sauce is thick. Just before using, stir in the oil and butter.

To make the Lasagne

Cook the lasagne, a few at a time, in salted, boiling water for about 4 minutes. Drain, and put a layer into a well buttered casserole or fireproof dish.

Add a layer of mozzarella cheese, then a layer of sausage and a layer of hard boiled egg.

Sprinkle with grated Parmesan and ricotta cheese and moisten with some of the tomato sauce.

Continue in layers, finishing with a good thick layer of grated Parmesan. Dot with butter and bake in a moderate oven,

350°F., Gas Mark 4 for about 30 minutes.
Serve with a green salad.

Spaghetti with Tomato Sauce and Olives

Spaghetti con Salsa di Pomidoro e Olive

Tomato sauce No. 2
  (see page 84)
12 oz. spaghetti
butter

12-16 large black olives
2 tablespoons (2½ T) olive oil
grated Parmesan cheese

Prepare the tomato sauce. Cook the spaghetti as on page
Pit and halve the olives. Sauté for 2-3 minutes in a little olive
oil.
Drain the spaghetti, put into a hot serving dish and add a
generous nut of butter. Pour the tomato sauce over and
arrange the olives on top.
Serve hot with grated Parmesan cheese.

Spaghetti Bolognaise

This popular dish consists of spaghetti with a good meat sauce.
The recipe for the sauce is on page 81.
Cook the spaghetti in the usual way, pour the sauce over and
sprinkle generously with grated Parmesan cheese.

Pizza

Like Pasta, a whole book could be written on Pizzas. The word 'pizza' literally means a pie and as a very general description, a pizza is made with a bread dough, spread with a mixture of tomatoes, mozzarella cheese, anchovies etc. and baked in a hot oven. It should be eaten freshly baked, accompanied by a red wine or beer.

Pizzas can be small, enough for an individual portion and served as an antipasto or large, served as a main meal.

Pizzas, like so many other Italian specialities, vary from one province to another. In Rome, the pizza filling generally consists of onion, rather than tomato. The Neapolitan pizza is perhaps the most famous and consists of a thin bread dough, smothered with a mixture of tomatoes, cheese, herbs and anchovies. In Genoa, the base is a bread made with oil and salt and is very good eaten with cheese.

In most Italian towns there are Pizzerias where pizzas are baked to order in the traditional wood-fired brick ovens and this seems to give them their unique taste.

Basic Pizza Dough

8 oz. (2 cups) flour
1 teaspoon salt
$\frac{1}{2}$ oz. compressed yeast

$\frac{1}{4}$ pint ($\frac{1}{2}$ cup) tepid water
1 tablespoon ($1\frac{1}{4}$ T) oil

Sift the flour and salt into a warmed bowl. Mix the yeast smoothly with the water, add the oil and pour into the flour. Mix to a smooth dough.

When it is pliable and leaves the sides of the bowl clean, turn on to a floured working surface and knead until the dough is smooth and elastic, probably for about 5-6 minutes.

Shape into a ball, put into a lightly oiled bowl, cover, and leave in a warm place until doubled in size.

SPAGHETTI BOLOGNAISE

Pizza with Olives and Herbs

Pizza con Olive e Erbe

This is a different kind of pizza in as much as it has a base of pastry instead of yeast dough and it is cooked in a flan ring or pie plate. It is best to cook the pastry partly first, so if you use a pie plate or sandwich tin the pastry can be removed at this stage and the cooking finished on a baking tin.

Pastry
8 oz. (2 cups) flour
$\frac{1}{2}$ teaspoon salt
4 oz. ($\frac{1}{2}$ cup) lard or other
   cooking fat
2 eggs

Filling
3 tablespoons ($3\frac{3}{4}$ T) olive oil
2 onions, peeled and chopped
   finely
1 clove garlic, crushed
1 large can Italian peeled
   tomatoes (about $2\frac{1}{2}$ lb.)

2 tablespoons ($2\frac{1}{2}$ T) tomato
   purée
2 teaspoons dried oregano
2 teaspoons chopped fresh
   basil or 1 teaspoon dried
1 bay leaf
2 teaspoons sugar
1 teaspoon salt
freshly ground black pepper
fresh herbs, as available
pitted green olives

Make the pastry in the usual way, but use the beaten eggs and water as required for mixing. Roll out and line an 8 inch round baking tin, flan case or pie plate. Put some beans or crusts of bread in the bottom and bake in a moderate oven 375°F., Gas Mark 5 for 15 minutes.

To make the filling
Heat the oil in a pan and cook the onion and garlic until the onion is soft and transparent but not coloured. Add the coarsely chopped tomato and the liquid from the can, tomato purée, spices, sugar, salt and pepper.
Bring to boiling point, lower the heat and simmer very gently, uncovered, for about 45 minutes, stirring occasionally.
Remove the bay leaf, check the seasoning and pour into the pastry case.
Sprinkle with coarsely chopped fresh herbs and a few drops of oil. Arrange the olives on top and bake in a moderate oven 350°F., Gas Mark 4 for 10-15 minutes.

INDIVIDUAL PIZZAS (*Photograph: The Fruit Producers' Council*)

Tuna and Pear Pizza

Pizza con Tonno e Pere

$\frac{1}{2}$ lb. basic pizza dough,
  (see page 72)
olive oil
1 can (7-8 oz.) tuna
1 Spanish onion, peeled and
  chopped
2 ripe dessert pears, peeled,
  cored and chopped

1 can (about 8 oz.) Italian
  peeled tomatoes
$\frac{1}{2}$ teaspoon oregano
salt, black pepper
anchovy fillets
pickled walnuts or black
  olives

Knead the risen pizza dough lightly, place on an oiled baking
sheet and flatten into a round about 10-11 inches across. Brush
lightly with oil.
Drain the oil from the tuna into a pan, put the onion and pears
into the oil and cook for a few minutes. Add the flaked fish
and tomatoes and cook slowly, without a lid on the pan, for
about 25 minutes or until most of the liquid has evaporated.
Add oregano and seasoning to taste.
When the filling is cool, spread it over the dough. Top with
anchovy fillets and garnish with slices of pickled walnut or
olives.
Leave in a warm place for about 15 minutes to prove.
Bake in a hot oven 425°F., Gas Mark 7 for about 15 minutes.
Serve hot.

Noodles with Cream

Tagliatelle alla Panna

1 lb. green ribbon noodles
2 oz. (4 T) butter
2 egg yolks
4 oz. (1 cup) grated Parmesan
  cheese

6 tablespoons (7$\frac{1}{2}$ T) double
  (heavy) cream
freshly ground black pepper
extra butter and grated cheese

PIZZA WITH OLIVES AND HERBS

Cook the noodles in salted, boiling water until tender, but firm. Drain thoroughly and put into a large hot serving bowl. Add egg yolks, butter and cream and toss the noodles lightly until the heat has 'cooked' the eggs and cream. Add pepper and serve with extra butter and cheese.

Noodle Ring with Meat Sauce

Tagliatelle alla Sugo di Carne

2 tablespoons ($2\frac{1}{2}$ T) oil
1 onion, peeled and chopped
1 clove garlic, crushed
$\frac{1}{2}$ lb. (1 cup) minced (ground) raw beef
1 tablespoon ($1\frac{1}{4}$ T) tomato purée
1 green apple, cored and chopped (optional)

salt, pepper
$\frac{1}{4}$ teaspoon sugar
$\frac{1}{4}$ teaspoon dried basil
1 can (about 8 oz.) Italian peeled tomatoes
chopped parsley
12 oz. noodles

Heat the oil in a pan and fry the onion and garlic until the onion begins to brown. Add the meat and stir over medium heat for about 5 minutes.
Add tomato purée, apple, salt, pepper, sugar, basil and tomatoes. Cover, and simmer for about 40 minutes.
While the sauce is cooking, cook the noodles in salted, boiling water, drain, and pack into a well buttered ring mould. Keep hot.
When ready to serve, turn the noodle ring out on to a hot dish, pile the meat sauce in the middle and sprinkle with chopped parsley.

PEAR AND TUNA PIZZA (*Photograph: The Fruit Producers' Council*)

Spinach Gnocchi

Gnocchi Verdi

$1\frac{1}{2}$ lb. spinach
salt, pepper, nutmeg
butter
8 oz. (1 cup) Ricotta or cottage
   cheese

grated Parmesan cheese
2 eggs
3 oz. ($\frac{3}{4}$ cup) flour

Cook the well washed spinach with a little salt but no water.
Drain very thoroughly (this is important) and chop finely.
There should be at least 12 oz. spinach when chopped.
Put the chopped spinach into a pan with salt, pepper and
nutmeg to taste, a nut of butter and the Ricotta or sieved
cottage cheese. Stir over low heat for 5 minutes.
Remove from the heat, stir in the beaten eggs, 2 oz. ($\frac{1}{2}$ cup)
grated cheese and the flour. Mix well and refrigerate for
several hours.
Roll out on to a floured board and cut into rounds with a
$1\frac{1}{2}$-2 inch plain cutter.
Cook, a few at a time, in a shallow pan of gently boiling water.
In 4-5 minutes they will rise to the top. Remove carefully with
a fish slice or perforated spoon and put into a hot serving dish
which has been buttered and sprinkled lightly with grated
cheese. Keep hot while the remaining gnocchi are being
cooked, then sprinkle with melted butter and more grated
Parmesan cheese.

NOODLE RING WITH MEAT SAUCE (*Photograph: The Fruit Producers' Council*)

Sauces

Sauces are an important part of Italian cooking. Unlike the classical French sauces, most of them are simple, but they lack neither variety or originality.

There are a wide range of tomato sauces, all giving a rich red colour to the food, but in essence quite different.

Many meat sauces are used to give extra nourishment and flavour to pasta dishes, as for example the Bolognese sauce, and of course the famous Pesto, which is eaten with Pasta, especially by the Genoese.

The sauces which follow will be referred to in later recipes and others are given with their special dishes.

Bolognese Sauce

Ragu Bolognese

1 tablespoon ($1\frac{1}{4}$ T) butter
3 oz. bacon or uncooked ham, chopped
1 onion, chopped finely
1 carrot, peeled and chopped
1 stalk celery, chopped finely
$\frac{1}{2}$ lb. lean beef, minced (ground)

4 oz. chicken livers
1 tablespoon ($1\frac{1}{4}$ T) tomato purée
6 tablespoons ($7\frac{1}{2}$ T) white wine
$\frac{1}{2}$ pint (1 cup) stock or water
salt, pepper, nutmeg
$\frac{1}{8}$ pint ($\frac{1}{4}$ cup) cream or milk

Heat the butter in a pan and fry the bacon, onion, carrot and celery for about 10 minutes or until the vegetables are soft. Add the meat and when it has browned add the chopped chicken livers.

Cook for 2-3 minutes, then add tomato purée, wine and stock. Add a little pepper, grating of nutmeg and salt if required. Stir the mixture until it boils, then cover and simmer very gently for about 40 minutes, stirring occasionally.

Just before serving, stir in the cream or milk and check the seasoning.

Mayonnaise

Maionese

In Italy, mayonnaise is made with eggs and olive oil and perhaps a little lemon juice to sharpen it. If you wish to get the best results with your Italian dishes, do make your own mayonnaise.
Have all ingredients at room temperature and if by any chance, the mayonnaise curdles, it can be rectified. Break another egg yolk into a clean bowl, stir it a little, then add a spoonful of the curdled mixture.
When it is smooth, gradually add the the rest of the curdled mayonnaise.

3 egg yolks
8 fluid oz. (1 cup) olive oil

1 teaspoon salt

Put the egg yolks into a bowl standing on a non slip surface, or stand the bowl on a cloth.
Using a wooden spoon, stir for about 1 minute, then stir in the salt.
Add some oil, drop by drop, stirring vigorously until the mixture begins to thicken, then the flow of oil can be increased a little until eventually, it is running in a thin steady stream.
The mayonnaise should be thick and glossy, but if it becomes too thick, add a few drops of lemon juice or water.

Cheese Sauce

Salsa di Formaggio

1 oz. (2 T) butter
1 oz. (2 T) flour
$\frac{1}{2}$ pint warm milk (1 cup)
4 tablespoons (5 T) single (light) cream

2 tablespoons ($2\frac{1}{2}$ T) grated Parmesan cheese
2 tablespoons ($2\frac{1}{2}$ T) grated Gruyère cheese
salt, pepper

Melt the butter in a pan, add the flour and cook for a few minutes. Remove from the heat and add the warm milk gradually, stirring until the mixture is smooth.
Return to the heat, stir until boiling and boil for 3 minutes.
Add salt and pepper, then stir in the cream and grated cheese. If the sauce is not to be used at once, pour a little melted butter on top, to prevent a skin forming.

SPINACH GNOCCHI (*Photograph: The Fruit Producers' Council*)

Tomato Sauce

Salsa di Pomidoro

This is a very simple basic sauce which can be served with meat, fish or any kind of pasta.

2 lb. ripe tomatoes
1 small onion, peeled and
  chopped finely
1 carrot, peeled and chopped

1 stalk celery, chopped
1 teaspoon chopped parsley
salt, freshly ground pepper,
  sugar

Chop the tomatoes and put into a pan with the vegetables.
Add parsley, salt, pepper and a pinch of sugar. Simmer until
the tomatoes have cooked almost to a purée.
Pass through a sieve and correct the seasoning.
If a thicker sauce is required, it can be returned to the pan and
allowed to reduce until it is the right consistency.

Tomato Sauce 2

Salsa di Pomodoro

This is a useful sauce made with canned tomatoes.

2 tablespoons (2½ T) olive oil
1 small onion, peeled and
  finely chopped
2 cans Italian tomatoes (about
  1½ lb.)
2 tablespoons (2½ T) tomato
  purée

2 teaspoons chopped fresh
  basil or ½ teaspoon dried
  basil
1 teaspoon sugar
½ teaspoon salt
freshly ground black pepper

Heat the oil in a pan, add the onion and cook until the onion
is soft but not coloured.
Add the tomatoes, coarsely chopped, but not drained, and all
the other ingredients. Partially cover the pan and simmer over
very low heat for about 40 minutes, stirring occasionally.
Pass through a fine sieve or food mill and correct the
seasoning. This sauce should be fairly thick and is generally
used hot.

Neapolitan Tomato Sauce

Salsa Pizzaiola

This is another fresh tomato sauce flavoured with garlic and oregano and is a thicker sauce, the ingredients not being sieved.

1 tablespoon (1¼ T) olive oil
2 cloves garlic, crushed
1 lb. ripe tomatoes, skinned
salt, black pepper
1 teaspoon chopped fresh
  oregano or ½ teaspoon dried
1 teaspoon chopped parsley

Put the oil into a pan with the garlic and cook over low heat for a few minutes.
Chop the tomatoes into small pieces, add to the pan with salt and pepper to taste. Cook fairly quickly until the tomatoes have softened but they should not be pulped.
Add the oregano and parsley.

Pesto

Pesto alla Genovese

This is the famous sauce of Genoa, served with all kinds of pasta and as a flavouring in soups. A little stirred into Minestrone makes a world of difference to the flavour.
Fresh basil is essential for this sauce (real enthusiasts can grow it in a pot on a sunny window sill), and it needs pinenuts. It has been said that an imitation Pesto can be made with parsley and walnuts, but the flavour, of course, is quite different.

2 oz. fresh basil leaves,
  weighed after stripping from
  the stalks
2 cloves garlic
¼ teaspoon salt
2 oz. pinenuts
1½ oz. (scant ½ cup) grated
  Sardo or Parmesan cheese or
  equal quantities of both
3-4 tablespoons (3¾-5 T) olive
  oil

Chop the basil leaves and crush the garlic, then pound in a mortar with the salt and pinenuts until the mixture is reduced to a pulp.
Stir in the cheese.
Add the oil very gradually, a spoonful at a time and stirring well until the sauce has the consistency of a purée.

Fish

Most of the provinces in Italy have their own coastline and, after pasta, the sea is probably the source of the most important single category of food. There are red mullet, pinky octopus, huge tunny fish, scampi, boxes of writhing eels, crawfish, sea urchins (those purply black spiky balls) the ugly John Dory and fierce angler fish – to name but a few. Many of the fish which abound round the Italian coast are, of course, not available to us, but many of the Italian recipes are quite easily adapted. You will enjoy some of the fish soups and stews which are so typical of Italian fish cookery but the Italian housewife does not necessarily use complicated recipes and exotic sauces. Much of her fish cookery is done by the simple methods of frying, grilling (broiling) and baking and more often than not, the fish is served with a plain green salad. Cooked vegetables are very rarely served with fish.

Fish Stew

Burrida

This is a famous Genoese fish stew. The authentic ingredients are not possible for you to get in the ordinary way – even the names of some of the fish are frightening; scorfano, sea hen, octopus, pescatrice etc. – but you can really make an excellent fish stew with a variety of fish such as halibut, mackerel, lemon sole, scampi, conger eel etc.

4 tablespoons (5 T) olive oil
1 onion, peeled and chopped
1 small carrot, peeled and
  chopped
1 stalk celery, chopped
1 clove garlic, crushed
1 tablespoon ($1\frac{1}{4}$ T) finely
  chopped parsley
1-2 anchovy fillets, chopped

1 lb. fresh tomatoes, peeled
  and chopped or 1 small can
  (about 8 oz.) tomatoes
$\frac{1}{4}$ pint ($\frac{1}{2}$ cup) white wine
$\frac{1}{4}$ pint ($\frac{1}{2}$ cup) water
freshly ground pepper
$\frac{1}{2}$ teaspoon chopped basil
1 mackerel, cleaned and cut
  into thick slices

1 lemon sole, filleted and cut into strips

3/4-1 lb. eel, cut into 2 inch slices

salt

6-8 oz. filleted halibut, cut into strips

about 4 oz. prawns (shrimps) or scampi, frozen or fresh

4 slices French bread

Heat the oil in a large shallow pan, add the onion, garlic, celery, carrot, parsley and anchovy and cook for about 5 minutes.

Add tomatoes, wine, water, a little pepper and the basil. Cover and simmer for 15 minutes.

Add the prepared mackerel, sole, halibut and eel. Cover and simmer gently for 20-30 minutes, adding more wine or water if necessary.

Add the prawns or scampi, cook a further 5 minutes and correct the seasoning.

Fry or grill the slices of bread, put them into large deep soup plates and divide the fish stew evenly between the bowls.

Sole with Pinenuts

Sogliole con Pignoli

4 medium size soles

flour

salt, pepper

butter

2 tablespoons (2½ T) sultanas, or seedless raisins

2 tablespoons (2½ T) pine nuts

or blanched shredded almonds

1 small onion, peeled and finely chopped

¼ pint (½ cup) white wine vinegar

¼ pint (½ cup) water

Skin the soles on both sides and coat with flour to which a little salt and pepper has been added.

Heat some butter in a good sized sauté pan, put in the fish (if the pan is not large enough to take the four, cook half at a time) sultanas and pine nuts. Fry until the soles are browned on both sides and cooked through. Remove to a hot dish.

Put the onion into the pan, cook until it softens and begins to colour, add vinegar and water and cook for 10 minutes.

Correct the seasoning and pour the sauce over the fish.

Trout with Mushrooms

Trota con Funghi

In the Italian lakes and northern rivers there are excellent trout. They are usually cooked very simply – poached, fried or grilled (broiled). In this recipe they are fried and then just finished off in the oven.

4 trout
flour
salt, pepper
butter
olive oil
$\frac{1}{2}$ lb. mushrooms, sliced thinly

1 teaspoon lemon juice
3-4 spring onions (scallions), chopped
1 tablespoon ($1\frac{1}{4}$ T) fresh white breadcrumbs

Wash the trout, inside and out, but do not remove the heads and tails. Pat dry, season and coat with flour.
Heat about 2 tablespoons ($2\frac{1}{2}$ T) butter with 2 tablespoons ($2\frac{1}{2}$ T) olive oil. When it stops foaming, put in the trout and cook for 4-5 minutes each side. Remove and keep warm.
Put a little more butter into the pan, add the mushrooms, sprinkle with lemon juice and cook for 3 minutes shaking the pan frequently. Remove the mushrooms to a buttered, fireproof serving dish and arrange the trout on top.
Fry the onion and breadcrumbs for a few minutes adding a little more butter if necessary, then sprinkle over the trout.
Put into a fairly hot oven 425°F., Gas Mark 7 for a few minutes to brown on top or finish off under a hot grill (broiler).

Fish Cutlets with Sauce

Tranci di Merluzzo in Salsa

2 oz. (4 T) butter
4 cutlets, hake or cod
1 onion, peeled and finely chopped
2 tablespoons ($2\frac{1}{2}$ T) chopped capers
salt, pepper
$\frac{1}{4}$ pint ($\frac{1}{2}$ cup) dry white wine

1 tablespoon ($1\frac{1}{4}$ T) flour
$\frac{1}{2}$ teaspoon made mustard
2 teaspoons chopped parsley
2 eggs
lemon slices

Heat half the butter in a fireproof serving dish, put in the fish and sprinkle with the onion, half the capers, salt and pepper. Add the wine, cover and cook in a moderate oven 350°F., Gas Mark 4 for about 20 minutes or until the fish is cooked. Heat the remaining butter in a pan, add the flour, cook for a few minutes and remove from the heat. Add the liquor remaining in the dish in which the fish was cooked, return to the heat and stir until boiling.
Add mustard, parsley, remaining capers and beaten eggs. Reheat without boiling, correct the seasoning and pour the sauce over the fish. Garnish with lemon slices and capers.

Mixed Fried Fish

Fritto Misto di Mare

A Fritto Misto consists of a variable number of ingredients all fried separately. It may be a mixture of vegetables – fritto misto di verdure – or an assortment of meat and vegetables or, as in the following recipe, a variety of fish. The fish can either be coated with a thin batter – pastella – as shown in the picture or simply dusted with seasoned flour.
Choose a variety of fish, including prawns (shrimps).
Prepare the fish according to its kind, cut into small pieces, coat with batter or flour and fry in hot oil.
Drain well and serve with wedges of lemon and Tartar or Tomato sauce.

Frying Batter   Pastella
$\frac{1}{4}$ lb. (1 cup) flour
good pinch of salt
3 tablespoons ($3\frac{3}{4}$ T) olive oil
$\frac{3}{8}$ pint (1 cup) tepid water
1 egg white

Sift the flour and salt into a basin, add the oil and gradually add enough tepid water to make a smooth creamy batter. Leave to stand in a cold place for 2 hours.
When required for use, beat the egg white stiffly and fold it into the batter.

FISH CUTLETS WITH SAUCE

Eels

Anguille

Comacchio, in the Ferrara district of Italy, is built on sand and water, threaded with canals crossed by bridges – a sort of fisherman's Venice. Thousands of fishermen make their living fishing in the great lagoon, the Valli di Comacchio. Many varieties of fish are caught, but mostly eels. They are generally large and very firm and the Italian housewife cooks them in many ways – roasted, stewed and when very large, sometimes cut into thick slices, sandwiched between bay leaves and roasted on a spit.

They are also preserved by partly frying in olive oil, and then adding to the oil red wine, which has been boiled with salt and a little sugar, and leaving it all to marinate.

Stewed Eels

Anguille umido

$1\frac{1}{2}$ lb. eel
olive oil
1 onion, peeled and sliced
1 clove garlic, crushed
1 carrot, peeled and chopped
5-6 mushrooms, sliced

$\frac{1}{4}$ pint ($\frac{1}{2}$ cup) white wine
$\frac{1}{4}$ pint ($\frac{1}{2}$ cup) water
1 bay leaf
chopped parsley
salt, pepper

Skin the eels (the fishmonger will do this for you) and cut them into 2 inch lengths.

Heat some oil in a pan and fry the onion, garlic and carrot until soft. Add the mushrooms, cook for 2-3 minutes then add the eel, wine and water, which should just cover the fish. Add the bay leaf and a little seasoning.

Cover, and cook gently until the eel is tender (about 30 minutes). Serve sprinkled with chopped parsley.

FRITTO MISTO

Marinated Eel

Anguille Marinata

For the marinade
½ pint (1 cup) olive oil
2 onions, peeled and sliced
   thinly
2 cloves garlic, crushed
½ teaspoon thyme

2 bay leaves, crumbled
6 peppercorns
2 teaspoons salt
½ pint (1 cup) white wine
   vinegar

Heat the oil in a strong pan, add onion, garlic, flavourings and
salt and cook over moderate heat for about 8 minutes, stirring
frequently. When the onion is transparent, add the wine
vinegar and ½ pint (1 cup) water. Bring to boiling point, reduce
the heat and simmer, uncovered, for 20 minutes.

2 lb. eel
2 tablespoons (2½ T) lemon
   juice

flour
olive oil

Cut the skinned eel into 3 inch lengths and brush with the
lemon juice.
Coat with flour, then fry a few pieces at a time in hot oil for
about 4-5 minutes. As the pieces are fried, put them into a heat
proof dish.
When the marinade is ready, pour it – while still hot – over
the pieces of eel. Leave to cool, then cover and refrigerate for
at least 24 hours. To serve, arrange the pieces of eel on a
serving dish and moisten with a little of the marinade.

Tuna Mousse

Spuma di Tonno

1 can tuna (about 8 oz.)
1 tablespoon (1¼ T) butter
1 tablespoon (1¼ T) flour
¼ pint (½ cup) milk
1 egg
2 tablespoons (2½ T) chopped capers
1 tablespoon (1¼ T) chopped parsley

½ oz. (2 envelopes) gelatine
¼ pint (½ cup) hot water
¼ pint (½ cup) double (heavy) cream
lemon juice
salt, pepper

Drain the tuna fish and flake finely.
Make a sauce with the butter, flour and milk, add the egg yolk, capers, gherkin, parsley.
Dissolve the gelatine in the hot water and stir into the fish mixture.
Add the partly whipped cream and season to taste with lemon juice, salt and pepper.
Whisk the egg white stiffly and fold into the mixture. Put into a wetted mould or basin and refrigerate until set.
Turn out and garnish with gherkins.
Serve with a green salad.

Meat and Poultry

The Italians are not generally considered great meat eaters, but contrary to some criticism, veal is not the only meat available. The pork of Emilia, (including the sucking pig), the beef of Florence and other parts of Tuscany, and the lamb and kid of Rome are all excellent, but perhaps veal is the favourite. Vitello de latte comes from a calf only a few weeks old and which has been entirely milk fed. Vitello comes from calves up to six or nine months, and Vitellone is really baby beef.
Oxen are used for work in the fields and this is why some of the beef found in Italy is tough, but this meat can be used to make excellent beef stews. In fact, the Italians excel in making splendid dishes from the cheaper cuts of meat.
In Bologna and Tuscany poultry is particularly good and the Italians have a number of unusual ways of cooking it. In many recipes chicken breasts only are used, the rest of the bird made into soups and stews.

Escalopes

Escalopes of veal are thin slices cut from the fillet or top part of the leg and there are endless ways of serving them, all very delicious. Unfortunately, fillet of veal is very expensive so you will not find a great variety of dishes here using this particular cut. There are, however, recipes for very good veal dishes using the less expensive cuts of veal.
The following recipe is, perhaps the simplest and I think the best, method of cooking escalopes – with just a simple garnish of lemon and hard boiled egg.

96

Veal Escalopes

Scaloppe Milanese

4 escalopes of veal	butter
1 egg	1 hardboiled egg
salt, pepper	1 lemon
fine white breadcrumbs	

Ask your butcher to bat the excalopes very thinly. If you have
to do this yourself, put the meat between pieces of waxed
paper, and if you haven't a cutlet bat, use a bottle.
Beat the egg and season it with salt and pepper.
Dip the escalopes in the egg, then in breadcrumbs and press
them on well with a palette knife.
Heat some butter in a large frying pan and fry the escalopes
until golden brown on both sides, about 4-5 minutes each side.
Arrange on a hot serving dish and garnish with slices of lemon
and hard boiled egg.

Veal and Bean Stew

Spezzatino di Vitello ai Fagioli

$\frac{1}{2}$ lb. small white haricot beans, soaked overnight	salt, pepper
	1 wine glass white wine
2 tablespoons ($2\frac{1}{2}$ T) oil	4-5 tomatoes, peeled, seeded and chopped
1 tablespoon ($1\frac{1}{4}$ T) butter	
1 onion, peeled and chopped	$\frac{1}{2}$ teaspoon oregano
$1\frac{1}{2}$ lb. veal, cut into small pieces	stock
	chopped parsley
1 tablespoon ($1\frac{1}{4}$ T) flour	

Heat the oil and butter in a saucepan, add the onion and cook
until transparent.
Coat the veal with flour to which a little salt and pepper has been
added, put into the pan and brown on both sides. Add the
wine, let it bubble for a few minutes then add tomatoes, oregano
and beans. Add a little stock, bring to boiling point, then
cover and simmer gently until the beans are tender, adding
a little extra stock if necessary.
Correct the seasoning and sprinkle with chopped parsley.

Saltimbocca

This very simple, very Italian dish consists of thin slices of veal and ham cooked together with a sage leaf tucked in between. Prosciutto (raw ham) is generally used but thin slices of gammon or even cooked ham can be substituted. The word saltimbocca literally means 'jump in the mouth'.

Allow 2-3 small thin slices of veal for each person	sage leaves
an equal number and same size slices of thin raw or cooked ham	black pepper
	butter
	Marsala or white wine

Flatten the slices of veal as thinly as possible and sprinkle with a little black pepper. Lay a slice of ham on top and put a leaf of sage in between. Roll up lightly and secure with a toothpick. Heat some butter in a pan, put in the meat and brown well on all sides. Add a wine glass of Marsala, let it bubble for a minute or so, then cover the pan and cook for about 10 minutes, when the meat should be tender.
Arrange the meat on a serving dish, remove the toothpicks. Add a small nut of butter to the pan juices, boil up and pour over the meat.

Escalope of Veal Valdostana

Scallope di Vitello Valdostana

This is a dish for special occasions. The chef of the famous Tiberio restaurant in London gave me the recipe, which is a more elaborate version of Saltimbocca.

4 veal escalopes	1 small shallot, peeled and very finely chopped
flour	
salt, pepper	butter
butter	10 small button mushrooms
4 slices ham or tongue	1 rasher (slice) green bacon
4 very thin slices Gruyère cheese	6 tomatoes, peeled and seeded
black or green olives	1 stalk celery
	salt, pepper

VEAL AND BEAN STEW

Cook the shallot in a little butter until soft.

Put the mushrooms, bacon, tomatoes and celery through a mincer. Put into the pan with the shallots and sauté all together for about 15 minutes or until the mixture is dry. Add salt and pepper to taste.

Flatten the escalopes and coat with flour to which a little salt and pepper has been added.

Sauté in butter until they are firm and nearly cooked.

Spread the stuffing over each, cover with a slice of ham and top with a slice of cheese.

Arrange carefully in a buttered fireproof dish and put into a fairly hot oven 425°F., Gas Mark 7 until the cheese has melted and the meat has warmed through. Garnish with black or green olives and serve with a plain salad of lettuce or chicory with a little lemon dressing.

White truffles were originally included in the garnish, but, for obvious reasons they have been omitted from this recipe.

Fried Fillet Steaks Cacciatore

Bistecca Cacciatore

4 fillet steaks
1 tablespoon ($1\frac{1}{4}$ T) olive oil
salt, black pepper
1 wine glass red wine
2 tablespoons ($2\frac{1}{2}$ T) marsala
$\frac{1}{4}$ teaspoon crushed fennel

seeds or pinch powdered fennel
1 clove garlic, crushed
1 tablespoon ($1\frac{1}{4}$ T) tomato purée
chopped parsley

Fry the steaks in the hot oil, turning once and cooking according to your taste – rare, medium or well done.

Remove from the pan, put on to a hot serving dish, sprinkle with salt and black pepper, cover, and keep hot.

Add the wine, fennel and garlic to the juices left in the pan and let the mixture boil until it is reduced by about one third, add the tomato purée and stir until the sauce is smooth and of a creamy consistency. Add a little more wine if too thick.

Correct the seasoning, pour the sauce over the steaks and sprinkle with chopped parsley.

Serve with a salad.

Meat Balls with Spaghetti

Spaghetti alla Polpette

Polpette are best made with raw meat, but cooked meat can be used if you have some to use up. In this recipe, raw meat is used. It can be beef, veal, pork, or a mixture of meat.

1 lb. raw meat, minced
   (ground)
1-2 cloves garlic
2-3 sprigs parsley
thin slice lemon peel
1 apple, peeled and cored
   (optional)
1 large slice white bread,
   about $\frac{1}{2}$ inch thick, soaked
   in a little milk

1 egg
salt, pepper, nutmeg
oil for frying
tomato sauce, (see page 84)
12 oz. spaghetti, cooked (see
   page 61)
butter
chopped parsley

Put the meat, garlic, parsley, lemon peel and apple through a fine mincer or food mill.

Squeeze the moisture from the bread and add to the meat mixture.

Add the beaten egg and season with salt, pepper and nutmeg to taste.

Roll into balls with floured hands and roll the balls in flour, then fry until well browned. Drain on absorbent paper, put into the tomato sauce and leave to simmer very gently for about 20 minutes.

To serve – put the hot spaghetti into a serving dish, add a good nut of butter, arrange the meat balls on top, pour the tomato sauce over and sprinkle with chopped parsley.

Veal with Tuna Fish Sauce

Vitello Tonnato

This is a splendid cold supper dish for a party. It is best to start the preparation the day before, but the result is well worth a little extra trouble. The quantities given will be sufficient for 6-8 people.

$2\frac{1}{2}$-3 lb. boned leg of veal
6 anchovy fillets
2-3 bay leaves
1 onion, peeled and sliced
2 carrots, peeled and sliced
2 stalks celery, chopped

2-3 sprigs parsley
2 cloves
$\frac{1}{2}$ pint (1 cup) dry white wine
lemon and capers for garnish
salt, pepper

Tie the boned meat into a neat shape. Make little holes in the surface of the meat with a fine skewer and stick in little pieces of anchovy fillet.

Put the meat into a casserole, arrange the bay leaves on top and add the vegetables and herbs. Sprinkle with a little salt and pepper, add the wine and just enough water to barely cover the meat.

Put over low heat and bring to boiling point. Skim if necessary, then cover, and simmer very gently for $1\frac{1}{2}$-2 hours. When the meat is tender, remove from the heat and leave in the stock to get quite cold.

Tuna Sauce
1 can (7-8 oz.) tuna fish
6 anchovy fillets
1 teaspoon capers
2 tablespoons ($2\frac{1}{2}$ T) lemon
  juice

pepper
$\frac{1}{4}$ pint ($\frac{1}{2}$ cup) mayonnaise
  (see page 82)

Pound the tuna, anchovy fillets and capers to a smooth paste with the lemon juice and a little pepper. Add the mayonnaise and put into a blender if possible to make a smooth creamy sauce. Add a little strained veal stock if it is too thick.

To serve
Cut the veal into thin slices and arrange on a shallow oval serving dish. Mask with the cold sauce and garnish with slices of lemon and capers. Serve with a salad, see page 24 for Olive Salad, or page 29 for Rice Salad.

Stewed Shin of Veal

Ossobucco Milanese

2½-3 lb. shin of veal
flour
salt, pepper
2 oz. (4 T) butter
¼ pint (½ cup) white wine
1 lb. tomatoes, peeled and
    chopped

½ pint (1 cup) stock
3 tablespoons (3¾ T) chopped
    parsley
1 clove garlic, crushed
grated rind of ½ lemon

Ask your butcher to chop the veal into pieces about 2 inches thick. Coat them with flour to which a little salt and pepper has been added.
Heat the butter in a pan, brown the pieces of veal, then stand them upright in the pan so that the marrow will remain in the bone.
Add wine, cook for 10 minutes, then add stock and tomatoes. Cover, and cook over low heat for about 1½ hours.
Mix the parsley, garlic and lemon rind together and sprinkle on top of the dish before serving.

Serve with Risotto alla Milanese, see page 65.
This is traditional, but if you like to be adventurous try the recipe on page 66 for Risotto alla Arancia. It is very good with Ossobucco.

Veal Kidney with Marsala

Rognoni al Marsala

1 lb. veal kidney
1 tablespoon (1¼ T) flour
salt, pepper
butter
1 onion, peeled and chopped
    finely
1 clove garlic, crushed

¼ lb. bacon, cut into fairly
    thick pieces
8-10 button mushrooms,
    sliced
6 tablespoons (7½ T) Marsala
1 tablespoon (1¼ T) brandy

Remove fat and skin from the kidney, cut out the hard core, wash and pat dry. Coat well with flour to which a little salt and pepper has been added.
Heat some butter in a sauté pan, cook the onion and garlic until the onion is translucent. Add the kidney and brown on both sides.
Add the mushrooms and bacon, cook for a few minutes, then add any remaining flour and the Marsala. Bring to boiling point, then reduce the heat and cook very slowly until the kidney is tender – about 25-30 minutes.
Add brandy and correct the seasoning before serving.

Liver in Wine Sauce

Fegato di Vitella con Vino

1 lb. calf's liver, cut into thin
    slices
flour
salt, pepper
2 tablespoons (2½ T) olive oil
1 medium size onion, peeled
    and finely chopped

2 oz. Prosciutto or cooked
    ham, chopped
3 tablespoon (3¾ T) finely
    chopped parsley
⅛ pint (¼ cup) dry red wine

Coat the liver with flour to which some salt and pepper has been added.
Heat the oil in a pan, put in the liver and brown on both sides. Avoid overcooking – it should only take about 4-5 minutes. Remove the liver to a serving dish and keep warm.

Put the onion, ham and parsley into the remaining oil and cook until the onion is soft and golden brown. Add the wine, stir well and boil until the sauce has reduced a little. Check the seasoning, pour over the liver and serve at once.

Rabbit Stew

Coniglio al Marsala

1 small aubergine (egg plant)
salt, pepper
1 oz. (2 T) butter
2 rashers (slices) bacon,
   chopped
1 stalk celery, chopped
1 rabbit, jointed
4 tomatoes, peeled and
   chopped

1 clove garlic, crushed
1 sprig thyme, salt, pepper
1 small glass Marsala
stock
1 small red or green pepper,
   seeded and cut into strips

Cut the unpeeled aubergine into about 1 inch squares, sprinkle with salt and leave to drain for about 1 hour.
Heat the butter in a saucepan, add bacon, celery and joints of rabbit and fry until lightly browned.
Add tomatoes, garlic, thyme and seasoning. Add Marsala and allow it to bubble until the quantity has reduced by half, then add enough water or stock to barely cover the rabbit. Bring to boiling point, skim if necessary then cover and simmer for about $\frac{1}{2}$ hour.
Add the drained aubergine and cook for another 20 minutes, then add the strips of pepper.
Check the seasoning before serving.

Pork Stew

Casoeula

In and around Milan, this is a favourite way of cooking pork.

1 oz. (2 T) butter
1 onion, peeled and chopped
3-4 oz. bacon, chopped
½ lb. carrots, peeled and cut
   into thin rounds
1-2 stalks celery, chopped
1½ lb. lean pork
½ lb. cotechino (or other Italian
   salame)

piece of pork or bacon rind
1 bay leaf
salt, pepper
1 tablespoon (1¼ T) flour
½ pint (1 cup) white wine
1 firm white cabbage (2-2½ lb.)

Heat the butter in a large heavy pan, put in the onion, bacon, carrots and celery and cook until the onion is soft and brown. Add the pork and cotechino, cut into pieces and the bacon rind. Add the bay leaf and a little salt and pepper and sprinkle with the flour.
Stir in the wine and a little water if there is not enough liquid to barely cover the contents of the pan.
Cover, and simmer gently for 1 hour.
Wash the cabbage, cut it into four pieces and cook in salted, boiling water for 10 minutes. Drain, and when the meat has cooked for 1 hour, put in the cabbage and cook a further 30 minutes. Before serving, remove the bay leaf and piece of bacon rind and correct the seasoning.

Pork Chops with Marsala and Fennel

Costa di Maiale al Marsala e Finocchio

4 pork chops
salt, pepper

butter or other fat for frying
1 clove garlic, crushed

2 tablespoons (2½ T) dry red wine
¼ pint (½ cup) Marsala

1 tablespoon (1¼ T) tomato purée
½ teaspoon fennel seeds

Trim the chops, season with salt and pepper and brown on both sides in the hot fat. Reduce the heat and cook gently till the meat is tender – about 20 minutes. Remove from the pan and keep hot.
Put the garlic into the fat remaining in the pan and allow it to brown, stir in all the other ingredients.
Cook for about 6 minutes, then correct the seasoning and strain over the chops.
Serve with pasta or with a green salad.

Chicken Breasts with Asparagus

Petti di Pollo alla Asparagi

4 chicken breasts
salt, pepper
flour
2 eggs
2 oz. (½ cup) grated Parmesan cheese

2 tablespoons (2½ T) butter
2 tablespoon (2½ T) olive oil
about 12 cooked asparagus spears

Flatten the chicken breasts a little, season with salt and pepper and coat with flour.
Beat the eggs in a shallow dish and add half the grated cheese.
Put in the chicken breasts one at a time and brush thoroughly with the egg and cheese mixture.
Heat the butter and oil and fry the chicken until golden brown on both sides – about 8-10 minutes.
Drain, and arrange a few asparagus spears on each one.
Sprinkle with the remaining cheese and put under a hot grill (broiler) for a few minutes until the cheese melts and browns.

Desserts

The pastry shops in Italy offer an impressive variety of creamy cakes and pastries, all very highly decorated. Yet while Italian pastry cooks are still famous, it is a fact that Italian housewives do not set great store on serving puddings and sweets. They rely much more on fresh fruit and cheese. The creamy cakes are eaten in large quantities in coffee bars and sweet biscuits and macaroons – which the Italians are said to have invented – are often served with aperitifs.
No book on Italian cookery, however, would be complete without reference to some of the traditional desserts, many of which are simple to make and delicious to eat.
There is a special light, crumbly pastry used for fruit flans and Ricotta cheese is used in a number of sweet dishes.
The famous Mont Blanc is only one of the many sweets made with chestnuts and, of course, Zabaglione, made with eggs and Marsala, cannot be omitted. Italy has always been famous for its ice cream and it is alleged that it was the Italians who introduced it to Europe but so many people, these days, prefer to buy ice cream that recipes for this have not been included.

Cream Cheese Dessert

Crema di Mascherpone

2 eggs
2 oz. ($\frac{1}{4}$ cup) sugar
8 oz. (1 cup) cream cheese, sieved

1-2 tablespoons ($1\frac{1}{4}$-$2\frac{1}{2}$ T) Kirsch or brandy
sponge fingers (ladyfingers)

Separate the eggs, beat the yolks with the sugar and sieved cheese until light.
Add Kirsch.
Beat the egg whites stiffly and fold into the cream.
Pile into individual dishes and surround with the strawberries. Serve with sponge fingers.

112

Stuffed Peaches

Pesche Ripiene

3 oz. ($\frac{1}{2}$ cup) seeded or seedless
  raisins
3 tablespoons ($3\frac{3}{4}$ T) brandy
5 large ripe peaches

4 oz. macaroons
icing (confectioners') sugar
whipped cream
almonds

Put the raisins into a pan with the brandy, bring slowly to
boiling point, then leave to get cold.
Peel one of the peaches, remove the stone and put the peach
into a basin, with the macaroons. Pound well together, add the
raisins and brandy and a little icing sugar to taste. If the
mixture is too stiff, add a little more brandy.
Cut the four remaining peaches in halves, remove the stone
and sandwich the halves together again with the filling
between.
Put a whirl of whipped cream on top and finish with a
blanched toasted almond.

Caramel Oranges

Aranci Caramellizzati

5 oranges
6 oz. ($\frac{3}{4}$ cup) sugar
$\frac{1}{4}$ pint ($\frac{1}{2}$ cup) water

1 tablespoon ($1\frac{1}{4}$ T) Kirsch or
  Curaçao

Put the sugar and water into a pan, bring to boiling point and
boil briskly for 5 minutes. Add liqueur.
Remove the peel and all the white pith from four of the
oranges (a small sharp knife is best to use for this). Put the
oranges into the syrup and be sure they are well coated. Leave
them for 2-3 minutes, then remove on to a serving dish.
Peel the remaining orange very thinly, (use a potato peeler).
Remove all the white pith from the peel and cut it into small
match sticks. Blanch the peel for 5 minutes in boiling water,
then drain and put it into the syrup. Cook over low heat until
the strips begin to colour, then sprinkle them over the oranges.
Serve cold.

Cream Cheese Pudding

Budino di Riccotta

This delicious pudding is made with Ricotta cheese. Cream cheese is quite a good substitute, but as so many recipes call for Ricotta, you may like to make your own cream cheese. It will keep quite well for a few days and, apart from using it for cooking, it can be eaten alone with salt or sugar as you wish.

To make about 1¼ lb. you will need 4 pints (10 cups) of fresh milk. Put it into a large bowl and leave it to stand in a warm place for about ½ hour. Stir in 2 teaspoons rennet, mix well and leave again in a warm place until the curd has separated from the whey. This will take about 4 hours.

Turn it into a large piece of muslin (cheesecloth) and hang up to drain for 24 hours. It should then be ready for use, but stir the curd gently so that it is evenly drained.

Dry white breadcrumbs	2 tablespoons (2½ T) chopped
3 egg yolks	candied peel
4 oz. (½ cup) sugar	3 tablespoons (3¾ T) sultanas
8 oz. (1 cup) Ricotta or cream cheese	(sultana raisins)
2 oz. (⅓ cup) ground almonds	2 teaspoons grated lemon rind

Butter a 6 inch round, loose bottomed cake tin and coat generously with breadcrumbs.

Beat egg yolks and sugar well together until light and creamy.

Add cheese and all the other ingredients and mix well.

Turn into the prepared tin, smooth the top and bake in a moderate oven 350°F., Gas Mark 4 for about 30 minutes or until firm to the touch.

Leave to cool, then turn out and sprinkle with icing (confectioners') sugar.

Peach Gateau

Torta di Pesche

This delicious sweet makes good use of the luscious Italian peaches. Canned peaches could be used when fresh ones are out of season.

To peel fresh peaches, dip them into boiling water for a minute or two. The gateau consists of sponge cake layered with an Italian custard (crema pasticciera) and peaches and raspberries – a real party sweet.

Crema Pasticciera
2 oz. ($\frac{1}{4}$ cup) sugar
1 oz. (2 T) flour
2 egg yolks

$\frac{1}{2}$ teaspoon grated lemon rind
$\frac{1}{2}$ pint (1 cup) milk
$\frac{1}{2}$ oz. (1 T) butter
Marsala

Put the sugar, flour, egg yolks and lemon rind into a basin, add a little of the milk and whisk all very well together. Put the rest of the milk on to boil, and whisk into the egg mixture. Return to the pan, and whisk until the mixture thickens. Stir in the butter and 1 tablespoon ($1\frac{1}{4}$ T) Marsala, cover and leave to get cold.

For the sponge
3 eggs
3 oz. (6 T) sugar

$\frac{1}{2}$ teaspoon grated lemon rind
$2\frac{1}{2}$ oz. (5 T) flour
pinch of salt

Butter and line an 8 inch sandwich tin with buttered paper.
Separate the eggs, beat the yolks, sugar and lemon rind together until thick and light in colour.
Beat the egg whites stiffly and fold very lightly into the yolks.
Fold in the sifted flour and salt.
Turn into the prepared tin and bake in a moderate oven, 375°F., Gas Mark 5 for 15-20 minutes. Turn out on to a cooling tray and leave to get cold.

To assemble the Torta
Cut the sponge through into three slices. Spread the bottom with half the custard and arrange some peach halves and raspberries on top. Sprinkle with a few drops of Marsala. Cover with the second slice of sponge, spread with the rest of the custard and add more peaches and raspberries. Top with the third slice of sponge, sprinkle with Marsala and arrange the rest of the peaches and raspberries on top.

PEACH GATEAU

Chestnuts in Marsala

Castagne al Marsala

This is a favourite Italian dessert, suitable for special occasions. The chestnuts can be served hot or cold.

1 lb. chestnuts
½ pint (1 cup) Marsala
⅛ pint (¼ cup) red wine
2 tablespoons (2½ T) sugar

2 oz. (⅓ cup) sultanas
   (sultana raisins)
cream

Skin the chestnuts as for Mont Blanc, page 125, keeping the nuts whole.
Put the chestnuts into a pan, add sugar and wine to cover the nuts.
Simmer over low heat for about ½ hour, add sultanas and simmer until the chestnuts are tender and the wine syrupy.
Serve with cream.

Cream Cheesecake

Cassata Alla Siciliana

This Italian confection consists of a sponge cake layered with a delightful mixture of Ricotta cheese and chocolate with candied fruits or peel. The whole cake is then covered with more cheese or with chocolate butter icing.

1 sponge cake (approximately
   6 × 3 inches deep)
1¼ lb. Ricotta or cream cheese
6 oz. (¾ cup) sugar
1 tablespoon (1¼ T) curaçao or
   apricot brandy

2 oz. (2 squares) plain
   chocolate, cut into small
   pieces
4 oz. (1 cup) candied peel,
   finely chopped

Cut the cake horizontally into three layers.
If Ricotta cheese is used, rub it through a sieve, then mix the cheese and sugar and beat well. Add flavouring. Divide the mixture and put half of it aside in the refrigerator for coating. Add chocolate and candied peel to the other half and mix well. Put the bottom layer of sponge on to a serving dish, sprinkle

with a little liqueur and spread with half the cheese mixture.
Cover with the second slice and repeat the process, then cover
with the top piece of sponge and press all lightly together.
Sprinkle with a little more liqueur and leave to chill for as
long as possible.
Spread the top and sides of the cake with the chilled cheese
mixture and decorate as liked with whirls of cheese and strips
of candied peel.

Chestnut and Chocolate Gateau

Torta di Castagne e Cioccolato

4 eggs
8 oz. (1 cup) sugar
3 oz. (3 squares) plain
   chocolate
2 tablespoons ($2\frac{1}{2}$ T) strong
   black coffee
$\frac{1}{2}$ lb. chestnut purée

Filling
3 oz. (3 squares) plain
   chocolate

2 tablespoons ($2\frac{1}{2}$ T) strong
   black coffee
2 egg yolks
1-2 tablespoons ($1\frac{1}{4}$-$2\frac{1}{2}$ T)
   sugar
$\frac{1}{4}$ pint ($\frac{1}{2}$ cup) (heavy) cream
marron glacé

Butter and line 2 x 6-7 in. sandwich tins with buttered paper.
Separate the eggs, beat the yolks and sugar until thick and pale.
Melt the chocolate in the coffee and stir into the egg mixture.
Add chestnut purée and fold in the stiffly beaten egg whites.
Put into the prepared tins and bake in a moderate oven
350°F., Gas Mark 4 for about 35 minutes. Turn out carefully
and leave to cool.

To make the filling
Melt the chocolate in the coffee over gentle heat and stir until
thick and smooth. Add beaten egg yolks and sugar and stir
until smooth. Leave to get cold, then add the cream.
Sandwich the cakes with half the cream and use the rest to
cover the top. Decorate if liked with marron glacé.

121

Stuffed Figs

Fichi Riprene

There are wonderful figs to be found all over Italy, especially in August and September, when they are fully ripe.
As an antipasta, served with prosciutto, they are very popular, but in this recipe they are stuffed with a cheese filling and would be served at the end of the meal.

4 ripe even size figs
8 oz. (1 cup) Ricotto, cottage
  or cream cheese
1 large egg

2 oz. ($\frac{1}{4}$ cup) sugar
1-2 tablespoons ($1\frac{1}{4}$-$2\frac{1}{2}$ T)
  Kirsch or brandy
almonds

Wipe the figs and cut down into quarters, just enough to be able to open out the fruit – be careful not to cut right through. If using cottage cheese, it should be sieved. Add egg yolk and sugar to the cheese and beat all together until light. Add flavouring.
Beat the egg white stiffly, and fold lightly into the cheese mixture.
Put into the centre of the pears and if liked, an almond in the top. Chill before serving.

Italian Short Pastry

Pasta Frolla

8 oz. (2 cups) flour
3 oz. ($\frac{3}{8}$ cup) sugar
4 oz. ($\frac{1}{2}$ cup) butter, slightly
   softened

$\frac{1}{2}$ teaspoon grated lemon rind
2 large egg yolks

Sift the flour and sugar onto a working surface and make a
well in the centre. Drop in the butter, lemon rind and
unbeaten egg yolks and gradually draw in the flour, using the
tips of the fingers.

Mix to a firm smooth dough, kneading as little and as lightly
as possible. Wrap in foil and chill until required.

Pastry Twists

Cenci alla Fiorentina

*These simple little pastry twists are made in Tuscany — whence also
comes the best Chianti.*

*In this part of Italy the housewife is renowned for her somewhat austere
home cooking with no pretence to sophistication.*

$4\frac{1}{2}$ oz. (1 cup plus 1 T) flour
pinch of salt
icing (confectioners') sugar
1 whole egg

1 egg yolk
2 teaspoons rum
oil for frying

Sift 4 oz. (1 cup) of the flour, salt and 1 teaspoon icing sugar
into a bowl. Make a well in the centre, add the eggs and rum.
Using the tips of the fingers, draw in the flour until the
ingredients can be gathered up into a rough ball.

Sprinkle the rest of the flour on to a working surface and
knead for 10 minutes, or until the extra flour has been worked
in and the dough is smooth and shiny.

Wrap in foil and refrigerate for at least 1 hour.

Working with half the dough at a time, roll it out on a floured
board until paper thin. Cut into strips about $\frac{1}{2}$ inch wide and
6-7 inches long. Tie into little knots and fry 4-5 at a time in
deep hot oil until golden brown (1-2 minutes).

Before serving, sprinkle generously with icing sugar.

Mont Blanc

Monte Bianco

1 lb. chestnuts

6 oz. ($\frac{3}{4}$ cup) sugar

salt

$\frac{1}{4}$ pint ($\frac{1}{2}$ cup) double (heavy) cream

2 teaspoons Marsala or rum

marron glacé or grated chocolate

Score the chestnuts once or twice across the rounded side and boil for 15 minutes. Take a few at a time from the water and remove the outer and inner skin.

Put the chestnuts back into the pan, cover with fresh water and simmer for $\frac{3}{4}$-1 hour or until quite tender. Drain, add sugar and a pinch of salt and mash until quite smooth.

Put the chestnuts into a potato ricer or food mill. Hold it over the dish on which the sweet is to be served and press them through so that they form a mound on the dish. Put aside to chill.

Decorate with marron glacé or grated chocolate.

Zabaglione

This is a very simple and delicious sweet but it must be made carefully or it will separate when put into glasses.

4 egg yolks

3 oz. ($\frac{3}{8}$ cup) sugar

8 tablespoons (10 T) Marsala

Put the egg yolks and sugar into a bowl and whisk until the mixture is light and frothy.

Stand the bowl over a pan of hot water, add the Marsala and whisk for about 10 minutes until the mixture is really thick. Pour into glasses and serve at once, while still hot, with sponge finger biscuits.

If the Zabaglione is properly cooked there should be no clear liquid at the bottom of the glass.

Chocolate Pudding

Torrone Molle

This is a kind of nougat mixture which the Italian housewife serves as a sweet. It needs no cooking and is very simple to make but, if possible, make it the day before it is required.

4 oz. ($\frac{1}{2}$ cup) unsalted (sweet) butter
4 oz. (1 cup) cocoa
4 oz. ($\frac{3}{4}$ cup) ground almonds
4 oz. ($\frac{1}{2}$ cup) sugar

1 egg
4 oz. plain biscuits
icing (confectioners') sugar
whipped cream

Beat the butter and cocoa until soft, then add ground almonds.
Melt the sugar in a small pan with 2-3 tablespoons ($2\frac{1}{2}$-$3\frac{3}{4}$ T) water, add to the cocoa mixture.
Add the beaten egg and fold in the biscuits, cut into small pieces, but avoid crumbling the biscuits.
Put the mixture into a buttered ring mould or a small bread tin and leave to get quite cold and set.
Turn out on to a serving dish, sprinkle with icing (confectioners') sugar and serve sliced with whipped cream.

Chocolate Nougat

Torrone di Cioccolato

4 fluid oz. ($\frac{1}{2}$ cup) honey
$\frac{1}{2}$ lb. (1 cup) sugar
6 oz. ($1\frac{1}{2}$ cups) cocoa

2 egg whites
1 lb. finely chopped and browned hazel nuts

Line a shallow tin, about 10 by 8 inches, with rice paper.
Put the honey and sugar into a strong pan and heat until the mixture begins to colour.
Beat the egg whites stiffly and add to the honey.
Mix the cocoa with a little water and stir over low heat until quite smooth. Add the cocoa and nuts to the honey mixture and mix all well together.
Pour into the prepared tin and leave to set.
Cut into pieces for serving.

Index

Figures in italics refer to illustrations

Anchovies on toast 20
Antipasti
  artichoke hearts 16
  French beans 17
  mushrooms in marinade 17
  spinach stuffed eggs 15
  tuna stuffed tomatoes 15
  zucchini with walnuts 16
  see also Salads
Antipasti, hot
  anchovies on toast 20
  cheese and anchovy sandwiches 18
  cheese and anchovy savouries 19
  chicken livers on toast 19
Antipasti platter 14
Artichokes
  baked 53
  stuffed 40, *42*
Artichoke hearts 16
Asparagus
  Italian 57
  with cheese 57
  with mayonnaise and hard boiled
    eggs *58-9*
Asti Spumante (wine) 11
Aubergines
  salad 28
  stuffed 52, *54*
  with cheese and tomato 44
Aurum (liqueur) 12

Basil 10
Bay leaves 10
Beans with sweet peppers 49
Bel Paese cheese 9
Bolognese sauce 81
Borage 10

Cabbage with bacon and fennel 45
Cacciatore, fried fillet steaks 101
Caciocavallo cheese 9
Caramel oranges 113, *114-15*
Cauliflower with tomato and cheese
  56
Cheese and anchovy sandwiches 18
Cheese and anchovy savouries 19
Cheesecake, cream *119*, 120
Cheese sauce 82
Cheeses, Italian 8-10
Chestnut 125
  and chocolate gateau 121
  in Marsala 120
Chestnut soup 33
Chianti 11
Chicken
  breasts with asparagus 111
  livers on toast 19
Chicken cream soup 34, *35*

Chocolate nougat 126
Chocolate pudding 126
Cinzano 12
Consommé with pasta and chicken
  livers 34
Cotechino 14
Courgettes *see* zucchini
Cream cheese dessert 112
Cream cheese pudding 116

Desserts
  caramel oranges 113
  chestnuts in Marsala 120
  chestnut and chocolate gateau 121
  chocolate nougat 126
  chocolate pudding 126
  cream cheesecake *119*, 120
  cream cheese dessert 112
  cream cheese pudding 116
  Mont Blanc 125
  peach gateau 116-17
  stuffed figs 122, *123*
  stuffed peaches 113, *114-15*
  Zabaglione 125

Eels 92
  marinated 93
  stewed 92
Egg soup, ragged 32
Eggs
  spinach stuffed 15
  with spinach *55*, 56
Escalope
  of veal Valdostana 100
  veal 97

Fennel 10
Figs, stuffed 122, *123*
Fish
  cutlets with sauce 88, *90*
  mixed fried 89, *91*
  sole with pinenuts 87
  stew 86
  trout with mushrooms 88
Florence fennel 10
Fontina cheese 9
French beans 17
Fried fillet steak Cacciatore 101

Garlic 10
Gorgonzola cheese 9
Green peas with ham 53
Green peppers, stuffed 41
Green soup 36

Ham and pasta salad 21, *23*
Herbs and spices used in Italian
  cooking 10-11
Herb stuffed mushrooms *43*, 44

Italian short pastry 124

Lacrima Christa (wine) 11
Lasagne *Frontispiece*
  baked 68
Liver in wine sauce 108-9

Macaroni salad 22, *23*
Maraschino (liqueur) 12
Marjoram 10
Marsala (wine) 11
Martini 12
Mayonnaise 82
Meat and poultry 96-111
Meat balls with spaghetti 102, *103*
Milanese, risotto alla 65
Minestrone 37, *39*
  Milan 38
Mint 10
Mixed fried fish 89, *91*
Mont Blanc 125
Mortadella 13
Mozzarella cheese 9
Mushroom and prawn (shrimp)
  salad 25
Mushroom, herb stuffed 44
Mushrooms in marinade 17

Neapolitan tomato sauce 85
Noodle ring with meat sauce 77, *79*
Noodles with cream 76

Olive salad 24
Oregano, wild 10
Orvieto (wine) 11

Paradise soup 33
Parmesan cheese 8
Parsley 10
Pasta
  and chicken salad *23*, 24
  general rules for cooking 60-1
  selection of *63*
Pastry
  Italian short 124
  twists 124
Pavia soup 32
Peach gateau 116-17
Peaches, stuffed 113, *114-15*
Pecorino cheese 9
  Romano 9
  Sardo 9
Pesto 85
Piedmont rice 14, 62
Pizza 72, *74*
  basic dough for 72
  filling for 73
  pastry for 73

tuna and pear 76
  with olives and herbs 73, 75
Pork
  chops with Marsala and fennel
    110-11
  stew 110
Potato and tuna salad 20
Prosciutto 13
Provolone cheese 9

Rabbit stew 109
Ratafia (liqueur) 12
Red peppers 46, 47
Rice 62
  and green pea soup 36
  and scampi salad 21
  Piedmont 14, 62
  risotto dishes 64-7
  salad 29
Ricotta cheese 9, 116, 120
Risotto *Frontispiece*, 64
  alla Milanese 65
  with beans and bacon 67
  with ham and peas 64
  with orange 66
  with tuna 66
Rosemary 11

Sage 11
Saffron 11
Salad
  aubergine 28
  ham and pasta 21, 23
  macaroni 22, 23
  mushroom and prawn (shrimp) 25
  olive 24
  pasta chicken salad 23, 24
  potato and tuna 20
  rice 29
  rice and scampi 21
  scampi, apple and cheese 27, 28
  tomato and scampi 25, 26
  Zucchini 30

Salame 14
Saltimbocca 100
Sauce
  Bolognese 81
  cheese 82
  mayonnaise 82
  Neapolitan tomato 85
  Pesto 85
  tomato 84
  tuna 104
Scampi, apple and cheese salad 27,
  28
Soave (wine) 11
Sole with Pinenuts 87
Soup 31
  chestnut 33
  chicken cream 34, 35
  consommé with pasta and chicken
    livers 34
  green 36
  Milan Minestrone 38
  Minestrone 37, 39
  Paradise 33
  Pavia 32
  ragged egg 32
  rice and green pea 36
Soup pastas *Frontispiece*
Spaghetti
  Bolognaise 69, 71
  meat balls with 102, 103
  with tomato sauce and olives 69,
    70
Spinach Gnocchi 80, 83
Spinach stuffed eggs 15
Spinach with eggs 55, 56
Stewed Eels 92
Stracchino cheese 10
Strega (liqueur) 12

Tagliatelli *Frontispiece*
Tomato and scampi salad 25, 26
Tomatoes with olives 46
Tomato sauce 84

Trout with mushrooms 88
Tuna and pear pizza 76, 78
Tuna Mousse 94, 95
Tuna sauce 104
Tuna stuffed tomatoes 15

Veal
  and bean stew 97, 99
  escalopes 97, 98
  kidneys with Marsala 106-7, 108
  stewed shin of 105
  Valdostana, escalope 100
  with tuna fish sauce 104-5
Vegetables
  artichokes, baked 53
  artichokes, stuffed 40, 42
  asparagus with cheese 57
  aubergines, stuffed 52, 54
  aubergines with cheese and
    tomato 44
  beans with sweet peppers 49
  cabbage with bacon and fennél 45
  cauliflower with tomato and
    cheese 56
  green peas with ham 53
  green peppers, stuffed 41
  herb stuffed mushrooms 43, 44
  red peppers 46, 47
  spinach with eggs 55, 56
  tomatoes with olives 46
  Zucchini dishes 16, 30, 48-9, 50-1,
    52
Vermouth 12

Wines, with Italian meals 11-12

Zabaglione 125
Zucchini
  fried 52
  salad 30
  stuffed 48
  with ham 48-9, 50-1
  with walnuts 16